IMAGES
of America

VICTORIA MANSION

ON THE COVER: Victoria Mansion, built at the corner of Park and Danforth Streets in Portland, Maine, between 1858 and 1860, is shown here in a photograph dating to the end of the 19th century. Home to the Morse and Libby families into the 1920s, it was preserved as a museum in 1941 and has been open to the public since. The building has changed little inside and out since the time of its construction. (Courtesy of Victoria Mansion.)

IMAGES
of America

VICTORIA MANSION

Thomas B. Johnson and Timothy Brosnihan
Foreword by Earle G. Shettleworth Jr.

ARCADIA
PUBLISHING

ISBN 978-1-4671-0856-0

Published by Arcadia Publishing
Charleston, South Carolina

Printed in the United States of America

Library of Congress Control Number: 2022936196

For all general information, please contact Arcadia Publishing:
Telephone 843-853-2070
Fax 843-853-0044
E-mail sales@arcadiapublishing.com
For customer service and orders:
Toll-Free 1-888-313-2665

Visit us on the Internet at www.arcadiapublishing.com

This collection is dedicated to all those who worked together to create Victoria Mansion, as well as those who followed to preserve their work for future generations to enjoy.

Contents

FOREWORD

Victoria Mansion has long been recognized as an American architectural treasure—one of the nation's most well-preserved examples of an Italian villa–style residence of the 1850s. Few great houses of this period remain so intact in original design and furnishings. Narrowly saved from destruction in 1940, the house is now viewed as a monument to this country's cultural achievements in the pre–Civil War era.

The grand presence of the Morse-Libby House overshadows the fact that it was the home of two families for nearly 70 years before becoming a historic house museum in 1941. Its first owners, Ruggles and Olive Morse, resided there from 1860 to 1893. In 1894, the Mansion was acquired by Joseph R. Libby, whose family lived there until 1928. The last occupants were Libby's daughter Alice and her husband, Merle Brown.

As an 18-year-old summer reporter for the *Portland Evening Express* in 1967, I interviewed 88-year-old Alice Libby Brown about her life in the house. She recalled that her father instilled a sense of modesty in his children regarding their elegant surroundings. She and her two brothers and two sisters were raised in a religious atmosphere, where no unkind words were spoken. As soon as breakfast was over, her father would read from the Bible. The family then knelt and prayed.

The Libbys employed a cook, a maid, and a coachman. The coachman's duties included polishing the Mansion's many silver doorknobs and hinges. The downstairs parlor was reserved for formal occasions, while the upstairs one was used by the family. There, the Libby children had their Christmas tree.

Remembering the size of the Mansion, Alice Libby Brown told of an afternoon when she and her friends made fudge in the kitchen, her brother Harold held a debating society meeting in the library, and her mother hosted her sewing circle in the upstairs parlor. These activities occurred simultaneously without disturbing one another. Reflecting on such happy memories, she remarked, "It was a wonderful life. But after all, how could I take care of such a big house now."

—Earle G. Shettleworth Jr.
Maine State Historian

Acknowledgments

Victoria Mansion has attracted more than its fair share of saviors over the past 160 years, and all of us who enjoy the house in the present owe them a debt of gratitude. We now view the Libby family as the building's first preservationists, as they did so little to change it during their five-plus decades as stewards. Their legacy of care and generosity has only grown as children, grandchildren, and now great-grandchildren continue to return original furnishings.

Countless individuals have worked together since 1941 to save the building and return it to its former splendor. William Holmes deserves special recognition for purchasing Victoria Mansion with his own funds to preserve it, as does his sister Clara Holmes, who helped transform it into a museum. Arlene Palmer Schwind, a curator for more than 30 years, conducted much of the foundational research upon which our interpretation of the Mansion rests today, all while tracking down and negotiating the return of many original furnishings. Conservators, woodworkers, and artisans specializing in textiles, stained glass, stone, decorative plaster, and many other media have all lent their talents to the mix over the last 50 years, helping the Mansion evoke the past more effectively through their efforts in the present. We thank them all for their skill and dedication.

The authors are also sincerely grateful to two people who provided invaluable aid in the production of this book. Our thanks goes to Lauren Grant, who helped track down and digitize most of the images in this volume. Thanks also goes to Stacia Hanscom for her careful research, fact-checking, and copyediting.

Unless otherwise noted, all images appear courtesy of the Victoria Mansion's archives.

INTRODUCTION

Reporters took notice in the spring of 1858 when a grand new residence began to take form in a quiet neighborhood just outside of Portland, Maine's bustling downtown. Articles in the local newspapers dubbed the house "elegant," "superb," and "palatial," even before the wooden scaffolding encasing its rising walls was stripped away. "The Forest City," as Portland was sometimes called, contained a number of fine homes but nothing to touch this building for architectural impact.

The owners of this new palace, Ruggles and Olive Morse, were Maine natives who had made their way south over the course of the 19th century, landing ultimately in New Orleans, Louisiana, where Ruggles ran a number of the city's most luxurious hotels. Ruggles spent the two years prior to ground breaking laying plans for their summer retreat, first piecing together a double lot in a well-to-do neighborhood and ultimately commissioning New Haven, Connecticut, architect Henry Austin to draw up plans. Morse opened his purse and gave Austin the green light to think big. Austin, in turn, gave the Morses a house that would raise eyebrows even in the country's wealthiest enclaves: a boldly asymmetrical Italianate villa, clad in brownstone and adorned with richly carved architectural detailing and projecting piazzas and bays.

Even greater wonders greeted those lucky enough to be invited inside. To coordinate the house's lavishly appointed interiors, Morse hired 28-year-old Gustave Herter, a German-born designer who had immigrated to New York City a decade earlier. Herter, who would later pair up with his half-brother Christian to found the legendary Herter Brothers firm, was still relatively unknown in 1858, but already beginning to turn heads with his elegant and sophisticated furnishings. Herter cast a wide net for inspiration, bringing together a temporally and geographically eclectic mix of styles to produce something wholly new. Herter provided the overall controlling hand for the interior decoration at the Morse estate, creating an elaborate suite of furnishings and interior architectural ornamentation and selecting textiles, carpets, stained glass, and lighting fixtures, all of the highest quality and latest taste.

Equally important to the overall impact of the interiors was the work of Giuseppe Guidicini, an Italian-born decorative painter who worked both as a scenic artist for theatrical and operatic productions and as a decorator for some of the grandest theaters and opera houses built in the United States during the middle of the 19th century. Working with a small team of skilled artists, Guidicini executed an elaborate program of wall and ceiling paintings throughout the building, combining colorful canvasses painted with allegorical and mythological imagery with faux fabrics and woodwork and elaborate *trompe l'oeil*, or "fool the eye," detailing, painted on flat surfaces to appear three dimensional.

The combined efforts of these three creative geniuses—architect, decorator, and painter—flowed seamlessly together to form something truly astonishing, a monumental edifice with few peers anywhere on the continent. It is no wonder that the papers buzzed with details about the latest embellishments. As a reporter from the *Eastern Argus* enthused after a tour in June 1860,

"It is a palace good enough for a king- and most of that unfortunate class of human beings dwell in houses not half as elegant."

The Morses took up brief residence in the summer of 1860 but did not return until 1866, after the hostilities of the Civil War had ceased and free travel between the north and south resumed. For the next decade, they set up a pattern of sporadic occupation of their Portland mansion, mostly during the summer months, combined with longer stays in New Orleans, where Ruggles's myriad business interests were centered. Not until the mid-1870s, when Morse began winding down his career as a hotelier, did the house become more of a year-round residence. Into the 1890s, the house continued to serve the couple as a base from which they could quietly entertain friends and business associates and connect with their many Maine relatives.

When Ruggles Morse died in his Portland home in April 1893, his wife, Olive, began preparations for its sale. Few grand estates pass through such moments of transition fully intact. Relatives and creditors descend, and furnishings drift away. Remarkably, Victoria Mansion escaped this fate. This was due in part to the fact that Ruggles and Olive had no children; while Olive gave away a small number of pieces to nieces and nephews, the bulk of the house's contents remained in place. Equally important were the attitudes of the new owners, local merchant J.R. Libby and his wife Louisa, who bought the house fully furnished in 1894 and seemed to appreciate the grand sweep of its decorative scheme on its own terms. Beyond adding a few furnishings of their own, they changed very little.

From the get-go, the Libbys occupied the house more fully than the Morses ever had, making it their year-round residence and filling it almost to the rafters with people: their five children; at various points, their elderly mothers; and a revolving cast of aunts, cousins, and other relations. And yet they continued to live with and appreciate the Morses' things, even the most personalized of objects like glassware, silver, and porcelain marked out with the Morses' Gothic "M" monogram. The Libbys developed an affection for the house that ran deeper than sentimentality; they appreciated the building as a cohesive work of art. Happily for the house's future preservation, they passed this appreciation along to their grand and even great-grandchildren, who played a major role in the house's resurgence in the 20th century.

The house remained in Libby hands after J.R. and Louisa's deaths in 1917 and 1923. Their daughter Alice, who lived in the Mansion with her husband, Merle Brown, until 1928, was the last to move out. Over the ensuing decade, many of the more portable furnishings and decorative arts objects migrated to the homes of the five Libby children. By 1935, when a photographer working for the Historic American Buildings Survey came through to snap a series of interior shots, the rooms were mostly bare save for beds, built-ins, and window treatments. Various caretakers took up residence in the ell and kept an eye on the building, which was by then over 75 years old and beginning to show its age. By 1938, when a major hurricane tore through New England and badly damaged the central skylight, the building was in real peril.

But luck was on the building's side once more. Having become something of a burden to the Libby children, the house ultimately went on the market, where it failed to attract ready buyers. In time William Holmes, a retired New York educator looking to return to his native Maine, came through with a realtor and was immediately enamored. Learning that there was interest from a local petroleum company in tearing the house down and replacing it with a corner-lot filling station, Holmes stepped forward to purchase it with his own funds and set out to ensure its future preservation. After efforts to transfer the property to the Society for the Preservation of New England Antiquities fizzled, Holmes took a different tack. Partnering with his sister Clara, a teacher of interior design in New York City, he named the house "Victoria Mansion" in honor of Queen Victoria and opened it to the public as a museum in July of 1941. Holmes turned the property over to Clara, who in turn donated it to the newly incorporated Society of Maine Women of Achievement (SMWA), the earliest incarnation of the organization which continues to run the house as a museum to this day.

The SMWA, whose charter outlined a broad mission "to foster the cultural arts; to recognize worthy achievements of Maine mothers and daughters; [and] to preserve Victoria Mansion as a historic landmark and as the best standing example of Early Victorian art, architecture, and decoration," faced an uphill battle in caring for the deteriorating building. The tides did not truly begin to turn until 1971 when, with the help of Sen. Margaret Chase Smith, the house received National Historic Landmark designation and federal funds began to flow to help finance critical repairs. In 1985 the organization hired its first paid director, setting the museum on a path of increasing professionalization. Through the tireless efforts of trustee and curator Arlene Palmer Schwind, many original objects were located and secured from the Morse and Libby families. By degrees, the house slowly returned to its 1860 appearance both inside and out.

Entering through the front doors today, a visitor to Victoria Mansion encounters one of the most splendidly preserved Victorian interiors in America. Ninety-five percent of the original furnishings and decorative arts objects still occupy the exact same spaces in which they were placed in 1860. In many ways, the rooms give the appearance that time has stood still for more than 160-plus years. The truth, of course, is that it takes vision, effort, and money to stay the hand of time. But each generation seems to produce a handful of individuals "bitten" by this magnificent building, who willingly contribute toward its preservation for future generations.

Remarkable from the time it was constructed, Victoria Mansion has attracted photographers from its earliest days, looking to capture the pleasing lines of its architecture as well as the glories of its elaborate interiors. This book documents, through historical images, the whole arc of Victoria Mansion's history, both as a physical embodiment of the highest ideals of Victorian artistry and as an institution comprised of individuals working to care for and share it.

One

BEFORE THE MANSION

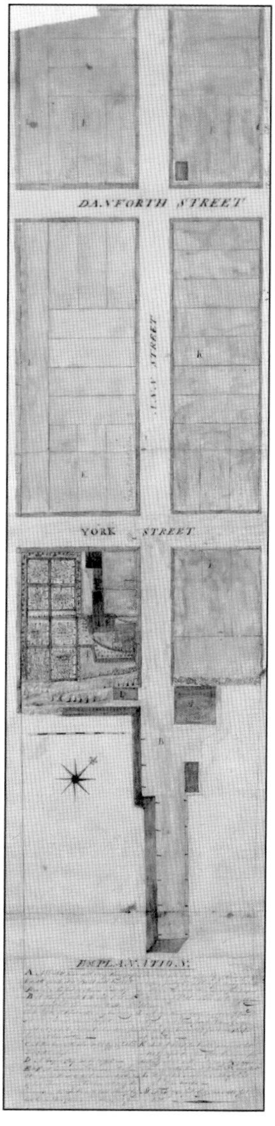

"A Plan of Ann [now Park] Street," dating from around 1802, shows the future location of the Mansion at the top of the image, on the northeast corner of Ann and Danforth Streets. By the end of the 18th century, the entire area was part of the vast estate of Scottish-born merchant and entrepreneur Thomas Robison. Robison, who arrived in Portland via Canada in 1783, launched an ambitious campaign to develop his landholdings, laying out Ann (now Park) Street from present-day Congress Street to the waterfront. Though Robison focused most of his energies on the commercial core of his property along the Fore River, he built the house shown here on the corner of Danforth and Ann Streets about 1785. He leased it to noted federal period cabinet maker John Seymour, who moved in with his family and produced furniture with his son Thomas on site. (Courtesy of Maine Historical Society.)

John Seymour, his wife, and six children immigrated from Axminster, England, to Portland in 1784, when son Thomas was 13 years old. Two years later, John sketched his new neighborhood; their home appears in the then-open area at the left of the drawing. In 1792, the family left for Boston, where father and son achieved further fame and financial success in their developing furniture business. (Courtesy of Maine Historical Society.)

Sixty-some years later, a fashionable neighborhood had developed in the formerly open fields surrounding this house. When the site was cleared for the construction of Victoria Mansion in 1858, the old Seymour house was moved to nearby Tate Street. This image shows a building that may in fact contain the "bones" of the Seymour house beneath its heavily altered façade. It was lost in the 1970s. (Courtesy of Maine Historical Society.)

In 1998 an archaeology project on the west lawn of the Mansion revealed the foundations and well of the Seymour House, fairly well preserved under three feet of fill added to the site in 1858. The remains were recorded and carefully re-covered and still exist to this day. (Courtesy of Independent Archaeological Consulting.)

In 1813, the finely proportioned McLellan-O'Toole House rose on the southeast corner of the Danforth/Park intersection. It is the last of the privately owned and occupied federal period homes in the neighborhood today, and is still lived in by family descendants. Beyond the addition of a projecting front entry, it looks today much as it did during the early 19th century. (Courtesy of Maine Historical Society.)

The area of Park and Danforth Streets began to develop as a fashionable residential neighborhood shortly after the Ann Street plan was done. At the northwest corner of the intersection, the Robison house was built around 1820 as a fine Federal brick mansion. Home to six-term Portland mayor Levi Cutter for almost 40 years, it was, by 1858, in use as a genteel boardinghouse. (Courtesy of Greater Portland Landmarks.)

Further up Park Street, the Presbyterians erected their Federal-style redbrick church building in 1829, and its steeple immediately became a prominent feature in the neighborhood. This c. 1920 view shows the church with its walls as originally painted gray, to mimic more costly granite. Today home to a Greek Orthodox denomination, it is the second oldest church building to survive in Portland and remains a local landmark. (Courtesy of Maine Historical Society.)

Park Street began to assume a more urban character when a company organized under the name Park Street Proprietary built a row of 14 attached townhouses between 1835 and 1838, part of a more ambitious development that failed due to a financial panic in 1838. Rarely seen outside of city settings, townhouses maximized access to increasingly precious street frontage by pulling neighboring buildings together. With each individual unit deep and tall rather than wide, townhouses allowed for the spacious accommodation of multiple families on a relatively small plot of land. Today, this handsome row exhibits several unaltered facades alongside those sporting later Victorian-era alterations. This 1970s view, taken near the corner of Park and Gray Streets, shows off an elegantly descending series of cast-iron balconies, which break up the broad expanse of the front elevation. (Courtesy of Greater Portland Landmarks.)

In 1851, the Carroll Mansion was completed on a slight promontory behind the Mansion's future site. A large house of robust Italianate style, it was designed by noted Portland gentleman architect/developer Charles Quincy Clapp as a wedding present for his daughter Julia and son-in-law John Bryce Carroll. Surrounded by elegant gardens and flanked by one of the largest brick carriage houses in the city, the Carroll Mansion set the tone for the development of the area as the city entered the 1850s. The buildings survive today after being converted to condominium residences in the 1970s. The gardens have given way to a swimming pool. This photograph predates its conversion and captures the vista enjoyed by the Morse and Libby families from the back of Victoria Mansion's lawn. The granite-capped retaining wall in the foreground divides the properties to this day. (Courtesy of Greater Portland Landmarks.)

This early-20th-century view of Victoria Mansion captures the original form of its near neighbor to the west. Built in 1833 for Portland merchant Oliver B. Dorrance, the Federal brick mansion received a lovely Greek Revival entry later in the 19th century. It still stands today, though its lines were somewhat changed with the addition of a fourth story during the 1910s.

By the 1870s, the Dorrance House was in use as a private day school. Run in association with nearby St. Luke's Episcopal Church, the St. Augustine's School for Boys took in small classes of pupils, promising "a careful attention to their physical and moral improvement." In this 1871 advertisement in the *Maine State Year-Book*, uniformed young men mingle near Victoria Mansion's front-drive gate.

Shortly after the completion of the Carroll Mansion, the last remaining unoccupied corner lot at the intersection of Park and Danforth Streets became the site of an imposing Greek Revival–style mansion built for Edwin Heckbert and later occupied by the Cutter family, shown here around 1910. As the neighborhood entered a decline in the 1930s, the house was converted to apartments, a role it fulfilled until its destruction by fire in the 1960s.

A pair of Italianate townhouses, built on Park Street in 1859 while the Mansion was rising on the opposite lot, also shared the neighborhood where the Mansion was to be built. Finely proportioned with well-appointed interiors, these houses fit nicely into the emerging upper-class enclave centered on Park and Danforth Streets. (Courtesy of Greater Portland Landmarks.)

Unfortunately, the double house came down in 1988, a fate shared by many of Portland's historic buildings in the constant churn of urban redevelopment. A fierce preservation battle, which included protests and arrests on the day the building was demolished, came to naught. In this photo, taken on June 20, 1988, a backhoe begins pulling down the brickwork of the building's ell. Happily, such losses have been rare in Victoria Mansion's immediate neighborhood. The parking lot which today sits on this building's footprint forms a notable gap in an otherwise intact 19th-century streetscape. In an unexpected silver lining, a large piece of Quincy granite recovered from the building's front steps proved to be a perfect match for a damaged stone in Victoria Mansion's perimeter fence and was later donated to aid in its restoration. (Courtesy of Greater Portland Landmarks.)

In this late-20th-century view, the McLellan O'Toole House is visible in the foreground, with later residential and industrial development stretching towards Portland harbor. In July 1866, a great fire began at a boatyard along this waterfront, spreading west (left) and fanning outwards as it marched across the commercial core of the city. In all, over 1,500 buildings were destroyed. By this time, Victoria Mansion stood at the corner of Park and Danforth Streets, and Ruggles and Olive Morse, visiting their summer home for the first time since the close of the Civil War, undoubtedly took in this view from the tower of their palatial new mansion as the city burned. Their residence, along with most others described in this chapter, survived thanks to the whims of the great conflagration, which skirted, but did not touch, their neighborhood.

Two

The Morses

In 1860, Maine natives Ruggles Sylvester Morse and his wife, Olive Ring Merrill Morse, returned to the state of their birth as a wealthy couple. They are shown here c. 1855. Outward trappings of success are evident: Ruggles wears what appear to be white silk pants, a silk scotch plaid vest, and a colorful cravat. Just above his arm at the left, a gold pocket watch nestles in the folds of the vest. Olive, more subdued in her dress of dark satin with velvet trims and a fine lace collar, nonetheless wears elaborate bracelets and rings, doubtless all of gold and precious stones. In her left hand, she clutches what appears to be a purse. All are subtle affirmations of their economic achievements and social standing.

Idealized oil portraits of Ruggles and Olive Morse were—and are—displayed in the Mansion's reception room. While acquiring a set of painted portraits was within the reach of even moderately well-to-do Americans by the second quarter of the 19th century, this pair, attributed to New Orleans artist Jacques Amans (1801–1888), was unusually fine. Olive holds a camellia, a winter-blooming plant adapted to mild southern climates like that of Louisiana, where she and Ruggles spent the better part of the year. Visitors waiting to meet the Morses would first have encountered their images staring down from perches on the reception room's elaborately decorated walls.

These *carte de visite* photographs date from the same approximate time as the oil portraits and show the couple in their forties in a current, if somewhat starker, reality. Ruggles Sylvester Morse grew up in the small rural community of Leeds, Maine, the third of nine children of Jonathan and Jane Libby Morse. Olive Ring Merrill grew up 30 miles to the south in Durham, Maine, the daughter of Jabez Merrill and Olive Mitchell Ring, who died soon after her birth. Neither Ruggles nor Olive were born into wealth. How they met is unknown. After publishing their marriage intentions in Portland, Maine, they married in Portsmouth, New Hampshire, in 1852.

Neither Ruggles's nor Olive's personal papers or diaries are known to have survived, leaving many questions about their inner lives unanswered. In many ways, the Mansion they would build in Portland, Maine remains the best document of their aspirations and accomplishments. Ruggles, in particular, "spoke" to visitors through its decorative embellishments. In the upper Stair Hall are four painted cartouches with the intertwined gold-leaf cipher reading "RSM" for Ruggles Sylvester Morse. Cyphers such as this are rarely if ever seen in American interiors, being more commonly encountered in European royal and ducal palaces as indications of nobility. Ruggles clearly intended to trumpet his arrival in high society and signal his wealth and sophistication. Having moved well past his humble roots, modesty was no longer a part of the bargain. There are no corresponding ciphers for Olive in the house.

Ruggles's climb to success was steep. Clearly energetic and ambitious, he left Leeds as a young man, striking out for Boston by the 1830s. His obituary suggests that he found work at the Tremont Hotel, shown here in an early lithograph. One of America's first luxury hotels, the Tremont opened young Morse's eyes to a lucrative career path providing accommodations to well-heeled travelers.

By 1838, the 24-year-old Ruggles Morse was living in New York City and likely working at the Astor House. Declining and a touch old-fashioned by the time this photograph was taken at the turn of the twentieth century, the Astor House had set a new standard for luxury accommodation when it opened in 1836, a pet project of tycoon and financier John Jacob Astor. While Morse's stay at the Astor House seems to have been brief, his experiences there formed another rung on the ladder of his success.

Through this view of New Orleans harbor in the 1840s, one can easily grasp the lure the city possessed for the ambitious young Ruggles Morse. Sitting near the mouth of the Mississippi, the country's greatest artery of commerce, New Orleans served as a nexus between the agricultural producers of America's heartland and consumers across the Atlantic world. As a hub of commercial activity, the city also attracted a large number of temporary inhabitants passing through on business, a key ingredient for success in the hotel trade. The imposing domed building dominating the skyline at the center of this image was the St. Charles Hotel, which appears to have provided Morse with his first job in the city. He joined tens of thousands of people from across the country and world who flocked to the city in the decades leading up to the Civil War in search of work and a chance at prosperity.

Completed in 1837, the St. Charles Hotel loomed over Canal Street, one of New Orleans' principal thoroughfares. Shown here in the late 19th century, after its reconstruction following a devastating 1851 fire, the St. Charles was a restaurant, barroom, and hotel in one, with 350 rooms for rent and a grand dining room seating up to 500 patrons. City directories indicate that Ruggles Morse was established in New Orleans and working as a clerk at the St. Charles by the late 1840s.

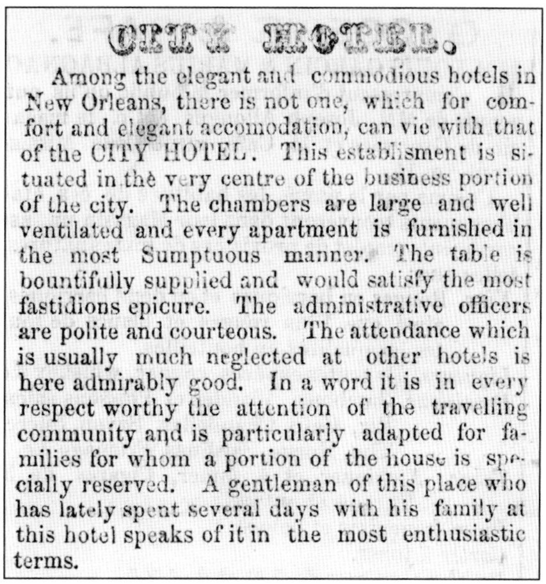

CITY HOTEL.

Among the elegant and commodious hotels in New Orleans, there is not one, which for comfort and elegant accomodation, can vie with that of the CITY HOTEL. This establisment is situated in the very centre of the business portion of the city. The chambers are large and well ventilated and every apartment is furnished in the most Sumptuous manner. The table is bountifully supplied and would satisfy the most fastidions epicure. The administrative officers are polite and courteous. The attendance which is usually much neglected at other hotels is here admirably good. In a word it is in every respect worthy the attention of the travelling community and is particularly adapted for families for whom a portion of the house is specially reserved. A gentleman of this place who has lately spent several days with his family at this hotel speaks of it in the most enthusiastic terms.

Morse graduated from clerk to manager and ultimately part owner of some of the most luxurious hotels in antebellum-, Civil War–, and Reconstruction-era New Orleans. The City Hotel welcomed both individual travelers and family groups. In this late-19th-century advertisement, clipped from a newspaper and hidden away inside a book in Morse's personal library for over 100 years, an anonymous reviewer gushes, "the table is beautifully supplied and would satisfy the most fastidious epicure."

Ruggles Morse took over management of the Arcade in 1852 and operated it as a hostel for commercial travelers, traders, and other gentlemen. It was noted at that time that "No person fond of good living and quiet comfort will ever regret ever having tarried with Mr. Morse at the Arcade Hotel."

Named for a massive interior arcade, which ran the full length of the building's rear facade, the Arcade was built in 1833 fronting busy Magazine Street. Its first-floor barroom, measuring 60 by 100 feet, served hotel guests as well as the general public. After a devastating fire in 1859, the Arcade was replaced with the five-story St. James Hotel, which Ruggles Morse managed in partnership with George C. Moore.

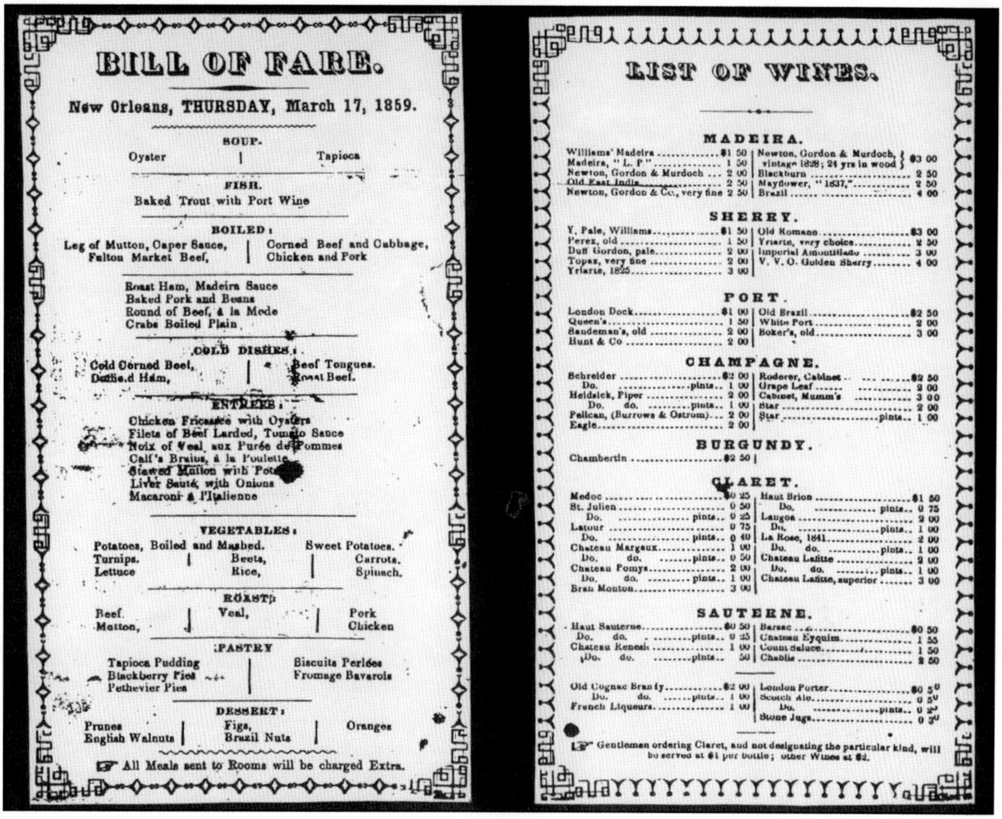

BILL OF FARE.

New Orleans, THURSDAY, March 17, 1859.

SOUP.

Oyster | Tapioca

FISH.

Baked Trout with Port Wine

BOILED:

Leg of Mutton, Caper Sauce,
Fulton Market Beef,
Corned Beef and Cabbage,
Chicken and Pork

Roast Ham, Madeira Sauce
Baked Pork and Beans
Round of Beef, à la Mode
Crabs Boiled Plain

COLD DISHES:

Cold Corned Beef,
Dellie.d Ham,
Beef Tongues.
Roast Beef.

ENTREES:

Chicken Fricassée with Oysters
Filets of Beef Larded, Tomato Sauce
Noix of Veal, aux Purée de Pommes
Calf's Brains, à la Poulette
Stewed Mutton with Pot…
Liver Sauté, with Onions
Macaroni à l'Italienne

VEGETABLES:

Potatoes, Boiled and Mashed. Sweet Potatoes.
Turnips. | Beets, | Carrots.
Lettuce | Rice, | Spinach.

ROASTS:

Beef. | Veal, | Pork
Mutton, | | Chicken

PASTRY

Tapioca Pudding
Blackberry Pies
Pethevier Pies
Biscuits Perlées
Fromage Bavarois

DESSERT:

Prunes | Figs, | Oranges
English Walnuts | Brazil Nuts |

All Meals sent to Rooms will be charged Extra.

LIST OF WINES.

MADEIRA.

Williams' Madeira $1 50
Madeira, "L. P" 1 50
Newton, Gordon & Murdoch ... 2 00
Old East India 2 50
Newton, Gordon & Co., very fine 2 50
Newton, Gordon & Murdoch, vintage 1828; 24 yrs in wood $3 00
Blackburn 2 50
Mayflower, "1837," 2 50
Brazil 4 00

SHERRY.

Y. Pale, Williams $1 50
Perez, old 1 50
Duff Gordon, pale 2 00
Topaz, very fine 2 00
Yriarte, 1825 .... 3 00
Old Romano $3 00
Yriarte, very choice 2 50
Imperial Amontillado 3 00
V. V. O. Golden Sherry 4 00

PORT.

London Dock $1 00
Queen's 1 50
Sandeman's, old 2 00
Hunt & Co 2 00
Old Brazil $2 50
White Port 2 00
Boker's, old 3 00

CHAMPAGNE.

Schreider $2 00
Do. .... pints.. 1 00
Heidsick, Piper 2 00
Do. do. .... pints.. 1 00
Pelican, (Burrows & Ostrom) ... 2 00
Eagle 2 00
Roderer, Cabinet $2 50
Grape Leaf 2 00
Cabinet, Mumm's 3 00
Star 2 00
Star .... pints.. 1 00

BURGUNDY.

Chambertin $2 50

CLARET.

Medoc $0 25
St. Julien 0 50
Do. .... pints.. 0 25
Latour 0 75
Do. .... pints.. 0 40
Chateau Margeaux 1 00
Do. do. .... pints.. 0 50
Chateau Pomys 2 00
Do. do. .... pints.. 1 00
Bran Mouton 3 00
Haut Brion $1 50
Do. .... pints.. 0 75
Laugoa 2 00
Do. .... pints.. 1 00
La Rose, 1841 .... 2 00
Do. do. .... pints.. 1 00
Chateau Lafitte 2 00
Do. do. .... pints.. 1 00
Chateau Lafitte, superior 3 00

SAUTERNE.

Haut Sauterne $0 50
Do. do. .... pints.. 0 25
Chateau Renesh 1 00
Do. do. .... pints.. 50
Barsac $0 50
Chateau Eyquim 1 55
Count Saluce 1 50
Chablis 2 50

Old Cognac Brandy $2 00
Do. do. .... pints.. 1 00
French Liqueurs 1 00
London Porter $0 50
Scotch Ale 0 50
Do. .... pints.. 0 25
Stone Jugs 0 30

Gentlemen ordering Claret, and not designating the particular kind, will be served at $1 per bottle; other Wines at $2.

Much of Ruggles Morse's hotel income derived from their dining rooms and bar service. This rare surviving copy of his menu offerings in both food and drink at the Arcade reveals the demands and extent of that facet of his business. While the City and the St. James Hotels welcomed accompanied women and families, the Arcade was reserved for the use of "gentlemen only" and indicated that "no arrangements have been made to accommodate ladies."

Shown here (the building at the center with two-story veranda and awnings on upper windows) in a c. 1870 photograph, the City Hotel offered 100 rooms for rent. Originally built in 1831, Ruggles Morse took over the lease in 1855, hosting a gala banquet for leading New Orleans citizens to celebrate the change in management. The 1860 federal census finds Morse in residence.

Here, a banner advertising "Wheelock, Finlay & Co., Druggists," hangs above the street in front of Ruggles Morse's St. James Hotel. Morse, whose business interests diversified as his fortune grew, was a silent partner in the firm's earlier incarnation, E.B. Wheelock & Company. He also traded in real estate both in Maine and Louisiana during the middle decades of the 19th century, invested in an insurance company in New Orleans, and was an investor in and managing partner of a luxury hotel in East Pascagoula, Mississippi. The Morses also participated actively in the grimmer side of the New Orleans economy, buying and selling at least 26 enslaved persons prior to the outbreak of the Civil War. By this time, New Orleans had become the central hub of the US domestic slave trade. Morse's participation in this trade included leasing space in both the City and Arcade Hotels for slave auctions during the 1850s.

By the time he stood for this portrait in a New Orleans studio in the mid-1850s, Ruggles Morse was a creature of two worlds. Raised in a quiet agricultural community of fewer than 1,500 residents, Ruggles achieved success in his new city by fully immersing himself in the culture of high society, attending balls, galas, and benefit dinners and even joining the elite Pickwick Club and at least two early Mardi Gras Krewes. His politics evolved in the crucible of antebellum New Orleans. In early January 1861, Maine-born Morse was one of nearly 200 officers of the Southern Rights Mass Meeting who crowded into the city's Odd Fellows hall to listen to fiery speeches calling for the succession of Louisiana from the Union. Remarkably, Morse managed to keep his business holdings relatively intact through the Union occupation of New Orleans between 1862 to 1865 and during the Reconstruction era that followed.

Ruggles's sister Caroline Morse Lothrop (1825–1901) bears a striking resemblance to her brother in this c. 1860 photograph. She was born and died in Leeds, Maine, but saw some of her children follow in the footsteps of their successful uncle and move south in pursuit of opportunity.

Shown here about the turn of the 20th century is St. Clair, a plantation once owned by Caroline's son Irving Lothrop (1856–1925). Situated in Plaquemines Parish, just below New Orleans, the plantation house exhibits some of the hallmarks of the French Creole style of architecture, including a complex roofline that flares to protect a wraparound porch.

Irving's older brother Elias Lothrop (1853–1919) graduated from Bowdoin College in Brunswick, Maine in 1875 before seeking his fortune in Louisiana. He purchased two plantations—Linwood and Greenwood—from his uncle in 1888. Morse himself had purchased these properties, situated in Plaquemines Parish just south of New Orleans, seven years earlier, an outlet for his entrepreneurial energies after his retirement from active hotel management. Elias is conspicuously absent from this early-20th-century family portrait, which contains four of his siblings, his in-laws, and at least two of his children. One wonders if he is standing behind the camera. From left to right are (first row, seated) Caro Lothrop and Florence Turner; (second row, seated) D.F. Lothrop, Caroline Lothrop, Olive Turner, and Dr. John Turner; (third row) Flora Higgins, Lucile Lothrop, Irving Lothrop, an unidentified young woman, and Ralph Lothrop.

Ruggles and Olive Morse maintained intimate ties with siblings, nieces, and nephews in the north as well as the south. Indeed, the draw of these family connections no doubt factored into their decision to summer in Maine. They were particularly close with niece Olive Morse Higgins (1855–1895), who was married in 1877 to James Appleton Morgan of New York City, a brief union that ended in divorce. Thereafter, she frequently stayed and traveled with the Morses. In many ways, Ruggles and Olive Morse treated Higgins, who was the daughter of Olive's sister Mary, like their own child. Ruggles served on the board of the Sylvester Larned Institute of New Orleans and no doubt helped find her a place there. She graduated in 1874. Sadly, she outlived her uncle by only two years. Her 1895 obituary described her "great literary ability" and "marked individuality."

Three

Building a Summer Palace

The Morses, steeped in the latest architectural, technological, and decorating trends through the management of hotels and extensive travel, engaged the best people of the time to ensure that their summer home would be fashionable, comfortable, and up-to-date in all its aspects. New Haven, Connecticut, architect Henry Austin was widely noted for his Italianate designs, and Victoria Mansion would prove to be one of his finest. (Courtesy of the New Haven Museum.)

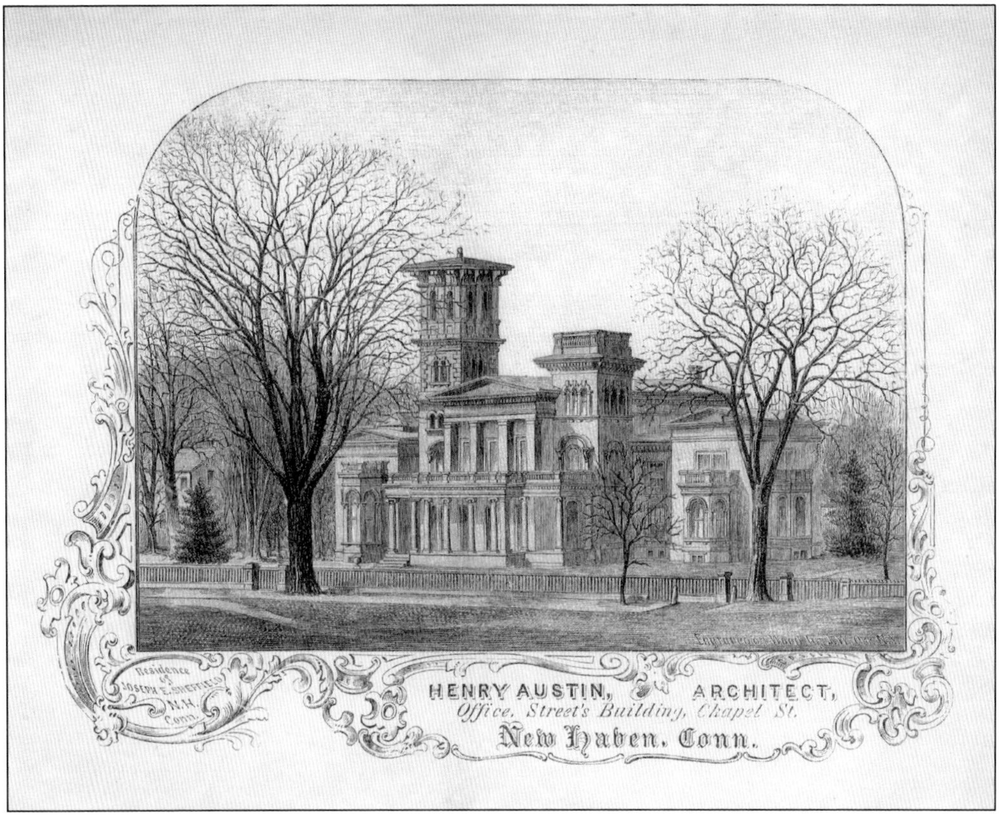

Henry Austin was drawn to a wide variety of Romantic architectural styles popular during the middle of the 19th century and was one of the leading proponents of the Italianate style in America. An advertisement from 1860 pictures a contemporary residence in New Haven that he had updated with Italianate elements similar to those he used at Victoria Mansion. (Courtesy of the New Haven Museum.)

Henry Austin's design for Ruggles Morse's summer home provided for granite retaining walls to elevate the house above street level; from the beginning, only a flat greensward of lawn with no ornamental plantings surrounded the house. In a very real sense, Austin was providing a raised plinth for the dramatic sculptural form of the Mansion itself.

Victoria Mansion was only partially complete in 1859 when William Willis published this engraving in his *Guide Book to Portland.* Likely composed from the architect's drawings—the proportions appear a bit off when compared with the actual building—this artist's rendering is the earliest image of Victoria Mansion. That it was included in a city guide before the Mansion was complete is a testament to the resounding architectural statement the building made.

This c. 1870s view looking west along Danforth Street sets Victoria Mansion in the context of its 19th-century neighborhood. The Mansion sits at the center of the photograph, its tower somewhat obscured by the forking trunk of one of the elms that lined the city's streets. Boldly asymmetrical, with projecting piazzas, portico and bay, and a lofty belvedere overlooking the harbor, the building stood out in a neighborhood of elegant but mostly boxy and prim residences.

Gustave Herter of New York City designed the interiors. A German immigrant, Herter left Europe in 1848 and first emerges in New York City directories in 1851. After a series of partnerships with others, Herter struck out on his own at age 28 in 1858. Victoria Mansion, which may well have been his first full domestic commission, contains his only interiors to survive fully intact. It is not known how Morse came into contact with Herter, but their collaboration was transformative for both parties. Morse acquired a house fully decorated and furnished in the latest taste, and between 1858 and 1860—the years he worked on Victoria Mansion's interiors—Herter's firm grew to employ 100 men and his stock of materials and furnishings at his New York factory climbed to a value of $125,000.

A more elusive craftsman who made a major contribution to the interior design of the Mansion was an Italian immigrant artist named Giuseppe Guidicini (c. 1806–1868). Working with a small troupe of assistants, Guidicini tackled the elaborate painted decoration in 14 of the Mansion's rooms as well as its soaring, three-story stair hall. Largely unknown today, Guidicini worked on a number of commissions in New York, Richmond, New Haven, and Cincinnati, none of which survive intact. A rare view of Tripler Hall in New York City, a theater decorated by Guidicini in 1850 and destroyed by fire in 1854, is one of the very few images documenting his work in other structures. Victoria Mansion's decorations are his only known surviving domestic wall and ceiling paintings and are proof of exceptional artistic talent.

This 1940s interior view of the Mansion captures some of the intricate interplay of Herter and Guidicini's contributions. Here, in close proximity, are carved wooden banisters and console brackets, cast-plaster door pediment and moldings, and trompe l'oeil painted decoration on the underside of the rising stair. Herter provided the overall controlling hand. His genius lay in his ability to harmonize arrangements of almost overwhelming complexity.

This photograph from the 1930s shows Guidicini's elaborate wall and ceiling fresco-type decoration. Herter accentuated the sumptuousness of the room with silk damask draperies and French *passementerie* trims in blue and metallic gold hanging from window cornices of burnished gold leaf. Note the use of etched and stained glass panels in the window sash and the glimpse of the original 1860 Scottish chenille carpet on the floor.

Guidicini's and Herter's mastery is again evident in the view of the Green Bedroom, taken in 1935. The trompe l'oeil framed wall panels were painted to imitate green silk damask, and a matching pattern was painted in ceiling reserves along with representations of the four seasons. Herter's deep green silk damask drapery with matching passementerie survives on the window and in the great half-tester bed reflected in the mirror.

Architect Henry Austin gave over valuable real estate in the core of the building to create a soaring space rising three stories past overhanging balconies. Dramatic whether viewed from above or below, the space's elaborately carved banisters and decoratively painted walls and ceilings were lit during the day by an overhead stained-glass skylight and at night by an elegant two-tiered gasolier.

This early 1900s view from the Dining Room across the central Stair Hall and into the Parlor offers a sense of Herter's ability to conceptualize interiors both in isolation, room-by-room, and in interaction with one another. Here, each room is distinct, with the heavily-carved chestnut and oak woodwork of the Dining Room contrasting with the light palette and delicate ornamentation of the hall and Parlor. Yet the alignment of their hanging lighting fixtures draws the eye from one space to the next and invites their contemplation as a whole. The effect is highlighted by two opposing mirrors in the Parlor and Dining Room. Monumental in scale and constructed with crystal-clear polished plate glass, the mirrors set up an optical illusion of infinitely repeated reflection.

Built at a time when stained glass was rarely encountered in domestic interiors, Victoria Mansion's more public spaces were punctuated with a series of colorful stained-glass windows. Crowning the lofty central hall, a 6-foot-by-26-foot skylight dazzled visitors with its prismatic colors and elegantly painted personifications of the four seasons.

The woodworkers in Herter's New York City manufactory were among the most skilled working in the United States. Made according to Herter's designs, the black walnut bookcases in Morse's library established a Gothic Revival theme in the room that was carried through the smallest details. Here, the library's decidedly Gothic gas lighting fixture echoes the pointed arch and quatrefoil motif of the bookcases in the intricate castings of its arms.

While virtually all of the Mansion's elaborate woodwork was created in Herter's New York City workshop, the front doors, shown here prior to restoration in the mid-1980s, were a notable exception. Charles H. Blake, a Portland woodworker whose stock-in-trade included counters, desks, and coffins, accepted a commission to construct the richly carved rosewood and walnut doors in 1860. Locals took notice. A reporter for the *Portland Transcript* wrote with palpable pride, "We frequently have the evidence presented to us that our mechanics and skilled artisans can execute as nice work, of all kinds, as can be done in any other city of the Union. An illustration of this fact may be seen at the shop of Mr. C.H. Blake on Union Street, who has constructed the front doors of the palatial mansion of Mr. R.S. Morse, on Danforth street. They are . . . as elegantly constructed as the case of a piano-forte."

Not everything within the house was as it first appeared. Herter and Guidicini delighted in fooling visitors with counterfeit marble, fabric, and woodwork. In the Dining Room, real oak and chestnut furnishings and paneling transition to a monumental *faux bois*, or false wood ceiling. Painted on plaster, the ceiling is a tour-de-force of the wood grainer's art, with precious figured woods such as birds eye and quilted maple imitated with astonishing fidelity.

Despite the removal of its furniture, the Parlor still held the power to dazzle in 1935, when photographers from the Historic American Building's Survey snapped this photograph. Textiles were among the most costly—and showy—aspects of the Mansion's interior décor. Here, the original red and pink chenille carpet and champagne silk window treatments with elaborate French tassels and trims are still on view.

The Morses acquired several works of art, including paintings and sculpture, from the estate of James Robb, a wealthy New Orleans financier who was forced to sell off much of his renowned collection in the aftermath of the financial panic of 1857. This included *The Iconoclasts*, a painting by Emmanuel Leutze (1816–1868), whose iconic painting *Washington Crossing the Delaware* graces nearly every US history textbook in publication. Herter incorporated the painting into the Parlor with an elaborate carved and gilt frame bearing Morse's cipher at its crest. Shown here hanging in the Portland home of one-time Victoria Mansion resident Ralph G. Libby, it returned to its rightful place on the Parlor wall in 1975, a gift of Harriet Payson Brazier Libby.

Many parts of the Mansion contain highly personal touches that speak directly to the public persona the Morses hoped to project. Here, *Columbia*, a personification of the United States of America, looks down on the hall below. Perched above state seals for Maine and Louisiana, this painting was long thought to indicate Morse's Unionist leanings. Records of his life in New Orleans, where he attended secessionist meetings before the war and helped memorialize Confederate general Robert E. Lee after it, complicate this simple narrative.

While the "public" areas of the house were limited to the first two floors, a third floor included a decorated guest bedroom, a 3,000-gallon cistern that captured rainwater for domestic use, a trunk storage room, and a decorated Billiards Room. Nearby, a winding staircase gave access to the fourth-floor level belvedere with spectacular views of Casco Bay.

A rear ell to the Mansion provided quarters for the staff and service areas such as kitchen facilities. The house design also provided storage and food preparation areas in the finished basement, alongside a private wine cellar that was protected by two stoutly padlocked iron sheathed doors. Nearby were three separate coal bays and a central furnace.

A granite paved driveway led to an adjoining Carriage House that included four horse stalls on the main floor and a finished living space above for a site caretaker. Also in the Carriage House was a privy for the use of the servants, accessible from an exterior door giving onto a slate-paved courtyard and work area to the rear of the Mansion.

Four

TECHNOLOGY

When constructed, the Mansion was a showcase of the latest developments in domestic technology. It is thought that one of the reasons Morse wanted to build on this particular site was the fact that some of Portland's earliest gas and sewer lines were laid under Park Street, shown to the left where it intersects with Danforth Street, allowing convenient access to municipal lighting and sewage disposal services. In this c. 1900 view, an early electric street lantern hangs suspended above the intersection.

Victoria Mansion was among the first houses in Portland to be fully piped for gas lighting from the time of its construction. All of the principal rooms, and most back areas, were equipped with gas lighting fixtures ordered from French, English, and American manufactories. The gasolier in the Turkish Smoking Room is gilt bronze with cut glass shades and is of British origin. The counterweights allow the fixture to be lowered for more directed light.

Radically new in its use were sets of push buttons that turned the lighting off and on. These buttons, installed at the entry to the Dining Room, were connected to a series of wet-cell batteries in the basement. While the mechanical components of the system are now lost, the batteries remained in the basement into the 1980s. The system was likely similar to those more commonly installed later in the 19th century, with one button to open the gas jet valves and create a spark and one to close the valves, thereby extinguishing the flames.

Gas sconces, like the pair seen here flanking the dining room mirror, provided additional lighting to supplement overhead fixtures. Indeed, the house's many mirrors amplified the rather dim light that gas provided. Dark for more than 100 years, the sconces picture here escaped electrification in 1902, when most of the house's fixtures were wired for incandescent bulbs.

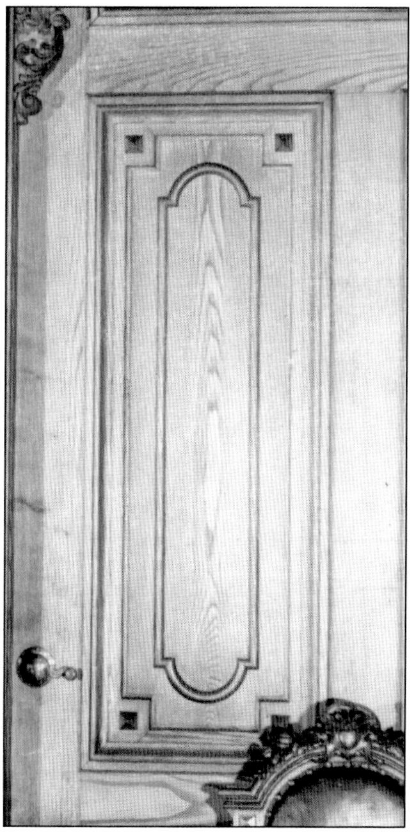

The main rooms of the Mansion were connected to call bells for summoning servants. The system was activated by wall sockets with silver handles attached to wires running through the walls and down to the basement. Through a series of relays there, the wires went up to the kitchen and tugged on individual bells on a call board indicating which room the call came from. The crank for the dining room call bell is visible in the lower-left quadrant of this photograph.

Hot and cold running water, found on both the first and second floors, was one of the house's true luxuries. Installed before the development of Portland's municipal water system, fixtures such as the one supplying the tub shown here were fed by rainwater collected in a large, lead-lined cistern on the third floor. Gravity provided all the force necessary to move water throughout the house's network of pipes. Hot water was heated in a boiler tank in the kitchen stove below and forced into select fixtures through the pressure generated by the third-floor cistern. A flush toilet—one of three in the house—is in a small room adjoining the bath. Flushed by a water tank hidden above the room's decoratively painted ceiling, it emptied into Portland's first municipal sewer on Park Street. A nearby sink is of delicately painted French porcelain.

No, it is not a ghost, but this remains one of the eeriest images ever taken in the Mansion. In 1935, the Historic American Buildings Survey (HABS) set out to document important historic structures throughout America. The shot of the Red Bedroom marble-topped walnut commode was set up straight on, with the camera on a tripod looking directly into the mirror. After timing the shot, the photographer stepped to the side to remove himself from the mirror reflection, but not before the aperture opened and briefly recorded his presence. What we see is a fleeting "ghost" of his image in the mirror. The double French porcelain sinks with hot and cold running water in the Red Bedroom exhibited the latest in hygiene technology. Guests staying in the room were treated to conveniences on par with those found in Morse's finest luxury hotels.

While physical evidence suggests that some cooking may have been done in the house's extensive and well-lit basement, the first floor of the ell served as the household's principal food preparation and staging area. The cast-iron stove shown here, a "Hot Air Range No. 4" made by Cyrus Carpenter of Boston, provided a low cooking surface for ease of placing large pots. The two ovens above could be preheated with the pull of an adjuster to divert hot flue gasses around the steel jacket enclosing the cooking space before they escaped out the chimney. For the generation that grew up in the waning days of open-hearth cooking, such ranges represented a revolutionary step forward in cooking technology. Originally, a copper boiler was attached to the stove for the heated water that was used here and throughout the house.

While the Morses may not have used the Mansion's coal-burning fireplaces during their summer stays, they were connected to chimney flues and fully functional. Indeed, the Libbys, who occupied the house after the Morses, regularly used the Reception Room fireplace, shown here, and others throughout the house to build cheery fires throughout the colder months. The house's principal source of heat, however, was a coal-burning furnace centrally placed in the basement with ductwork fanning out, octopus-like, to pass through the house's thick brick walls. Elegant cast-iron grates, like the one visible just to the left of the fireplace, allowed the rising heat to infiltrate the rooms. Coal provided an inexpensive way to heat a large house but had one major drawback: the dust generated as it was shoveled into bays in the basement. This dust traveled up through the ductwork to soil the house's furnishings and decoratively painted walls and ceilings. Carefully cleaning these deposits away has been the work of decades for museum conservators.

A prominent architectural feature, the tower also had a more utilitarian use as a passive ventilator for air throughout the house in the summer months. With windows open on the floors below, and the tower windows opened, a chimney effect was created that drew in cooler outside air and sucked warmer stale air up and out of the lower living areas. The wall and ceiling decorations mimic the interior of a draped-silk Bedouin tent.

Although the Libby family made few changes to the interior, they did add table lamps in several of the rooms, most of them fueled with gas siphoned from the ceiling gasoliers through rubber hoses. In this view of the library about 1895, the hose connecting the ceiling and table fixtures is clearly visible.

Five

THE LIBBYS

After purchasing the house fully furnished in 1894, Joseph R. ("J.R.") and Louisa Libby, their five children, and other relatives lived in it without any major changes, retaining the Morse interiors virtually intact during their occupancy. J.R. and Louisa had this portrait taken in 1895. They are seated on the Herter sofa in the Parlor, which still retained its 1860 satin upholstery and trims.

Born in 1845 in Buxton, Maine, Joseph Ralph Libby is shown here about 1880, during the early years of his success. Libby's life trajectory mirrored in some respects that of Ruggles Morse a generation earlier. Unsatisfied with a life divided between serving as a clerk in a small-town general store and helping out on his father's farm, he struck out for Boston at age 17, borrowing $5 to cover his traveling expenses. A brief stint as a clerk at a store on Tremont Row, just 100 yards from Morse's first post at the Tremont House hotel, was followed by several years spent as a traveling salesman in New York.

J.R. Libby fulfilled a life-long ambition in the fall of 1867, when he partnered with Boston merchant C.A. Vickery to open a store of his own in Portland, Maine. Situated on Free Street, just at the edge of the city's busy downtown, Libby's first store carried dry goods and operated out of the modest 2.5-story Greek Revival building pictured above. Ever restless, Libby stayed about a year before relocating to a more central location. Shortly thereafter, a generous offer from his previous employers enticed him to return to his former territories in New York as a traveling salesman.

J.R. Libby is shown here about 1890 (fifth from the left with a white hat) along with the staff of his fifth brick-and-mortar store, located in Biddeford, Maine. He took a long and winding path to arrive at this situation. In 1871, he partnered with A.S. and H.D. Mann to open a dry goods store in booming St. Louis, Missouri. The business flourished. When his partners offered to buy him out at a tidy profit, J.R., always looking forward to the next opportunity, took the money and headed back to Maine. He bought the successful F.A. Day store in the basement of Biddeford's old city hall before moving to this spacious first floor and basement layout in the new Biddeford Savings Bank building. This store was the first in the city to be electrified.

J.R. Libby married Louisa Larrabee in 1870. Louisa was born in Limington, Maine in 1845, mere miles from J.R.'s birthplace in Buxton. They met as youths at Limington Academy, forging an early bond that led J.R. to make courting visits between stints on the road. Louisa was bright and academically inclined, serving as an "assistant student" at Limington Academy and aspiring to attend Mt. Holyoke College, a dream that was never realized. She continued her studies at home in preparation for a teaching career. After her marriage, she devoted her life to charitable work and the care of her family. She was president of the Women's Home Missionary Union of Maine from 1908 to 1920 and helped her sons in the management of the department store during her later years.

J.R. Libby truly arrived in 1896, when he leased the lower three floors of the newly constructed Baxter Block on Portland's Congress Street. Shown here in a retouched photograph from that same year, the building became Libby's flagship store, a destination for the city's burgeoning middle class as well as visitors "from away." A banner flying over Portland's busiest thoroughfare declares the store the "Tourist's Headquarters."

J.R. Libby's department store was Portland's largest sales emporium. With over 40,000 square feet of sales space and 26 departments, it was lighted "by 660 electric lamps" and employed 200 in customer service. In 1917 a reporter from the *Portland Daily Press* enthused, "With its windows on three sides, the store is light, perfectly ventilated, and always attractive, a delightful place to shop in."

In this rare view inside the Libby store, taken around the turn of the 20th century, fabric, ties, and hosiery are piled high on shelves and displayed attractively in glass cases. Identified behind the counter from left to right are Ella Annette Salvas, Blanche Benoit Davis, and John Davis.

J.R. is shown with three of his employees outside the cashier's office. Above them hangs a sign reading, "Our Motto / He That Excels in Service / Wins Public Favor." That creed carried J.R. from his modest beginnings as a clerk and traveling salesman to the president of Maine's largest department store.

INFORMATION BUREAU
OF THE PORTLAND
Board of Trade
563
CONGRESS ST.
NICK
HUNT.
CIALTIES
CO. Ltd

Located just outside the busiest section of downtown Portland at the time of its construction, the J.R. Libby and Company department store helped pull the city's economic center of gravity to the north and west. Congress Street is bustling in this turn-of-the-20th-century view, with automobiles skirting streetcars in the center of the roadway and passersby stopping to admire the wares attractively arranged in the Libby store's expansive display windows. Department stores of the period went out of their way to attract and welcome women shoppers. The preponderance of women in this crowd of window shoppers is striking.

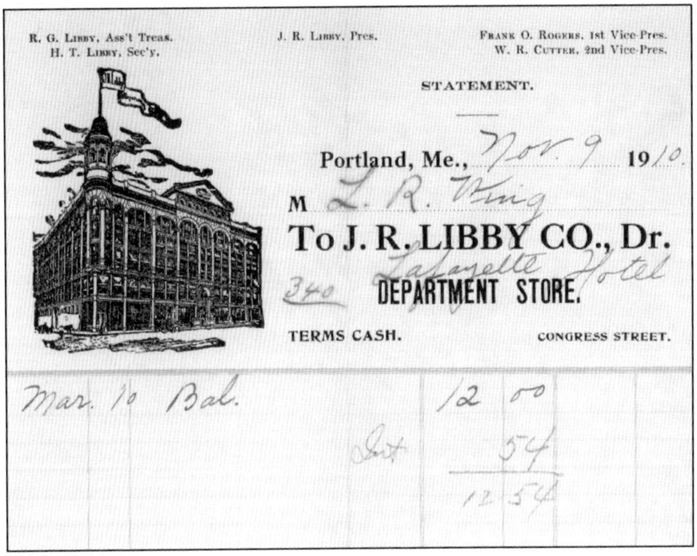

In this 1910 receipt for items delivered to the nearby Lafayette Hotel, Libby's Congress Street store is turned into a company emblem, with a larger-than-life pennant waving proudly above the corner turret. By this point, J.R. was joined in the management of the company by son Ralph G., who served as assistant treasurer, son Harold T., who served as secretary, and son-in-law William R. Cutter, who was second vice president.

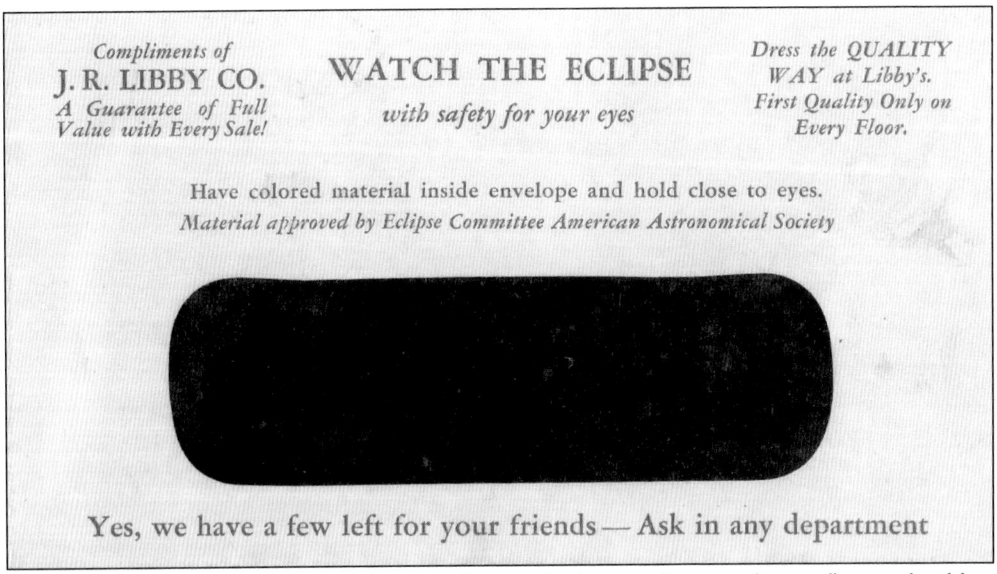

Cheap printing technology allowed for an explosion of ephemera from catalogs to flyers to booklets containing children's rhymes, all of which helped to spread the word about the Libby store. A 1917 *Portland Daily Press* article celebrating the J.R. Libby Company's 50th anniversary noted that Harold Libby took up the writing "ads" for the store, becoming an "acknowledged expert." Inexpensive giveaways, like this 1918 "Eclipse Viewer," wound up in the pockets of store-goers and helped subtly affirm the business's preeminence.

After J.R.'s death in 1917, management of the Libby Department Store fell to his son Ralph, who made history by accepting the very first delivery of cargo by air to Portland in July 1926. The cargo was a shipment of high-end dresses from New York City for the store's women's department.

The arrival of the air-mailed packages caused a near-sensation in downtown Portland. Here, onlookers crowd the sidewalks and cobblestone streets in front of the J.R. Libby store, jostling for a glimpse of the paper-bound merchandise. Others, likely store employees, peer down from the first-story windows above. In the days to come, a window display emerged with the delivery plane's route marked out on a map of the northeast.

The plane touched down in a grassy field on Portland's outskirts, where representatives from the J.R. Libby Store were on hand to transfer the packages to a waiting US Mail truck. Employees from the Libby store posed in front of the aircraft with the pilot and the mail truck driver. Where J.R. Libby was quick to electrify his stores and the first in Portland to motorize his fleet of delivery vehicles, son Ralph inherited his father's open-minded interest in new technologies. He is eighth from the left in this image.

The five Libby children in 1890. Clockwise from the left are Alice, Mary, Ralph, and Harold, surrounding their older sister Edith. Appreciation of education and Protestant religion were deeply ingrained in the Libby offspring, who started their day with a bible verse recited by their father over breakfast. The three Libby daughters later married in the Mansion. All five children would go on to successful lives and leave many descendants, many of whom maintain active connections to the museum to this day. They were, in many ways, the house's first preservationists.

In 1895, the house was featured in the publication *Beauties of Portland and Scenic Gems of Casco Bay*. It was considered one of the landmarks in Portland, a sight not to be missed when visiting the city. While keeping the interiors remarkably true to their 1860 appearance, the Libbys had nonetheless instituted minor changes in the rooms to make the house their own. In the Reception Room (upper left), the fringed armchair next to the fireplace has been brought downstairs from its original location in the upstairs sitting room, transforming what had been a rigidly formal space into a more comfortable living room. Across the stair hall in the Parlor (lower right), the room retains its formality, but a ruffled-shade kerosene lamp on a table at the far side of the marble mantelpiece introduces a more homely domestic note to the room, indicating its increasing use by the family.

Two views of the Parlor about 1895 record its original opulence. Some small additions such as the center table lamp, books, and pillows have been added by the Libbys to make the room more congenial to everyday use. Remarkably, the original 1860 satin furniture upholstery, elaborate window hangings, and carpet are still in use, testifying to the superlative quality of the Herter/Morse interiors. The two large paintings on either side of the door to the Stair Hall retain their original Herter-designed fames. The one on the right is *The Iconoclasts* by Emanuel Leutze (1816–1868), and the one on the left is *Jacob's Dream* by Luther Terry (1813–1869).

In this c. 1895 view of the Reception Room, the Libbys have added additional chairs and bric-a-brac to transform a once rigidly formal space into a family sitting room. Note the 18th-century "antique heirloom" banister-back armchair with added rockers in front of the window to the right, a symbol often chosen to signal deep American roots during the Colonial Revival era in the fourth quarter of the 19th century.

Thirty-five years of traffic in the Stair Hall had evidently taken a toll on the Morse-era chenille carpet. New England frugality and a demonstrated respect for the original contents of the Mansion led the Libbys to cover worn spots with oriental scatter rugs rather than replace the carpet wholesale. Several years later, they would add an oak hall tree to the rear of the hall; otherwise, the space remained much as it was when finished in 1860.

The Libbys were staunch supporters of temperance and prohibition. Maine's first prohibition laws went back to the 1840s and were written into the state constitution in 1885; in 1914, J.R. Libby was heading a subcommittee of the national Anti-Saloon League in the effort to take prohibition nationwide. The Libbys practiced what they preached, reputedly emptying the contents of the Morse wine cellar into the gutters upon purchasing the house.

One can almost feel the morning heat in this view of the house taken in the summer of 1910. Green- and white-canvas window awnings would have shielded the rooms from the full western sun in the afternoon. Potted tropical plants that ornamented the rooms during cooler weather have been moved out onto the front piazza.

Six

LIFE IN THE MANSION

After using the Mansion for years to escape the heat and disease then common to New Orleans's summers, Ruggles and Olive Morse used the house more regularly after Ruggles's semiretirement in 1874. This photograph, taken in the 1880s, shows the greying former businessman. There are no known photographs of Olive from this period.

This photograph taken in the Parlor is one of only two known images documenting Victoria Mansion's interiors as they were during the Morse occupancy. It hints at the opulence and sophistication of the room's original decor, with draperies festooned with swags of hand-wound silk flowers and the mantle shelf and pier table adorned with fine European glass and ceramics. Many of the furnishings shown here remain in the room to this day. Others, including the tall Bohemian ruby glass vases flanking the mantle clock, are still missing. The two lyre-back chairs in front of the fireplace were given by Olive Morse to Ruggles's Lothrop relatives. Their presence here allows us to date the photograph to 1894 or earlier. The chairs can be traced to an estate sale in Leeds, Maine, in 1969, after which the trail grows cold. It is hoped that they will someday be returned to their rightful place in the Parlor.

Late in the Morse's residency Portland experienced one of the most severe and destructive ice storms in its recorded history. This view up Park Street from the Danforth Street intersection (the Mansion is just out of the frame at the right) shows mature street trees whose limbs and branches have given way under the weight of their coating of ice. A period description called it "a most inconvenient storm." (Courtesy of Maine Historical Society.)

Ruggles Morse died in his Portland home in April 1893. A handwritten note, surviving today in the Mansion's collections, documents Olive's gratitude to an unidentified attendant for "kind assistance in the last sad services performed for her husband." Olive, who was 72 at the time of her husband's death, sold the house fully furnished within the year. She lived on for another decade, taking up residence in some of the city's finer hotels.

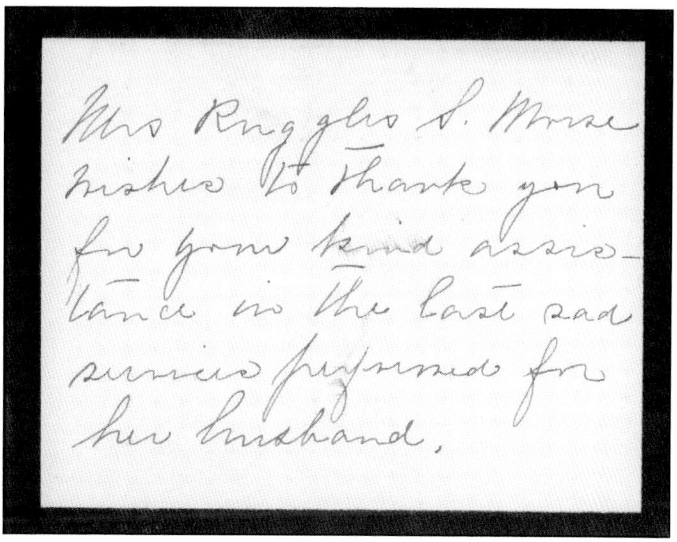

Mrs Ruggles S. Morse
wishes to thank you
for your kind assis-
tance in the last sad
services performed for
her husband,

After the relative quiet of the Morse occupancy, the house was to burst with life during the Libby ownership. Gregarious and family-centered, the Libbys took in both of their mothers in old age as well as assorted aunts, uncles, and other relations who came to stay at the Mansion at various intervals. Here, the family is seated in the Dining Room for Thanksgiving 1916. Louisa, looking at the camera from the right, and J.R., seated at the head of the table but obscured by a floral arrangement, preside over a gathering of 17 family members, including grandchildren.

In the preceding photograph, the table is set with the Morse-era porcelain, cut crystal, and silver that had been purchased with the Mansion in 1894. As thrifty New Englanders, the quality of the pieces was apparent to the Libbys, and they remained in use despite the fact that the porcelain and crystal were decorated with the monogram "M" and the silver was fully engraved "Morse." The majority of these pieces survive in the house today.

J.R.'s mother, Eliza Libby, lived with her son and his family at the close of her life during the winter of 1898–1899. Her obituary noted, "She has been an invalid for six years as a result of a shock," what we would call a stroke today. She died at the Mansion on January 25, 1899. This portrait was taken at the E. H. McKenney Studio in Biddeford, Maine.

Louisa's mother, Mary Thaxter Larrabee, moved in with the Libbys about 1900 and stayed for the final decade of her life. She slept in the converted Turkish Smoking Room, where she died on April 21, 1910.

In 1916, three generations of the Libby family pose in the Parlor. The children and their spouses stand behind the elder generation with J.R. (far right) holding his youngest grandson, Ralph Libby Jr. (1914–1995). Just to their right granddaughter Mary Chamberlain (1909–1954) sits on Louisa's lap.

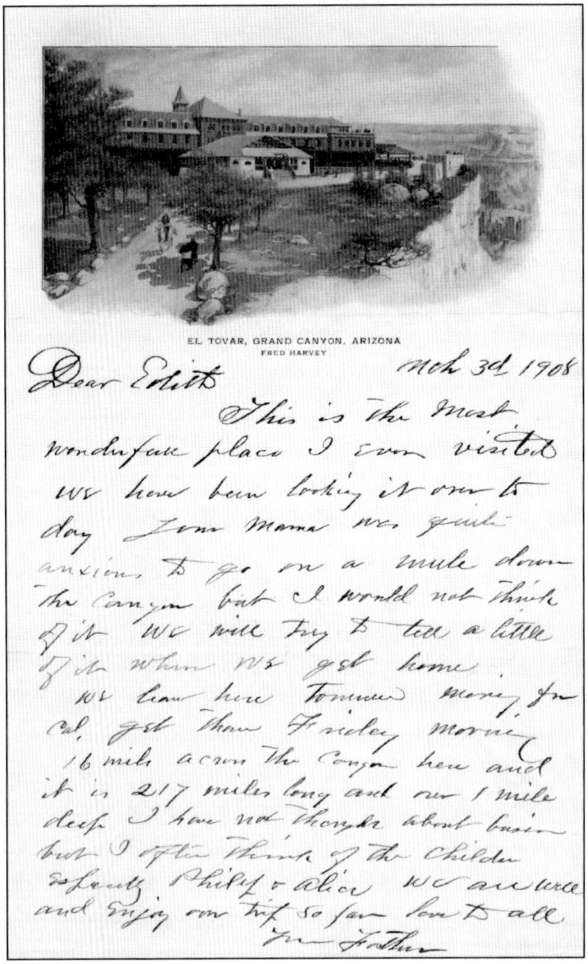

EL TOVAR, GRAND CANYON, ARIZONA
FRED HARVEY

Dear Edith Mch 3d 1908

This is the Most wonderful place I ever visited we have been looking it over to day Your Mama was quite anxious to go on a mule down the Canyon but I would not think of it We will try to tell a little of it when we get home We leave here Tomorrow morning for Cal. get there Friday morning 16 miles across the Canyon here and it is 217 miles long and over 1 mile deep I have not thought about business but I often think of the Children & family Philip & Alice We are well and enjoy our trip so far love to all

Your Father

J.R. Libby gradually ceded responsibilities for the day-to-day management of the department store to family members in the early 20th century, freeing him up to enjoy some of the fruits of his labors. In 1908, J.R. and Louisa traveled to the Grand Canyon in Arizona, which he called "the most wonderful place I ever visited" in a letter home to eldest daughter, Edith.

The couple traveled even further afield in 1911. Here, J.R. stands amongst the ruins of the Acropolis in Athens, Greece. Still intimately close with their adult children, J.R. and Louisa kept their family apprised of their travels through letters and postcards, sharing anecdotes and detailing their latest adventures.

More prosaic adventures took place closer to home. Here, Louisa Libby and her mother, Mary Thaxter Larrabee, with an unidentified child in tow, pick their way along Maine's rocky coastline. The state had, by this point, become a destination for tourists from all over the country, who were attracted to its wild and rugged beauty.

After the decease of their parents, the Libbys held on to family homesteads in Limington and Buxton, including the Larrabee house shown here. These properties became summer destinations for the family, with opportunities in the surrounding countryside for hiking, picnicking, and swimming.

For winter amusement, the city turned indoors. On February 7, 1896, the Portland High School Cadets donned military attire and hosted a dance at city hall, with special appearances by Portland's mayor and Maine's governor. Mary Louise Libby is thought to have attended. This dance card commemorating the event descended within her family.

Attendees used an attached pencil to mark their partner's initials next to dances, which included the "Two Step," "Virginia Reel," and "Portland Fancy."

The oldest of the Libby children resided at the Mansion for a relatively short amount of time. Edith, the eldest daughter, left shortly after her marriage to William Cutter of Boston.

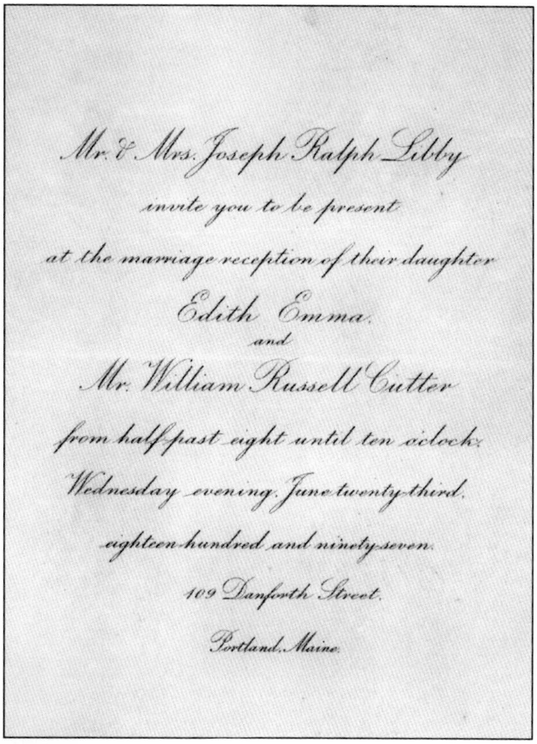

Mr. & Mrs. Joseph Ralph Libby
invite you to be present
at the marriage reception of their daughter
Edith Emma
and
Mr. William Russell Cutter
from half past eight until ten o'clock
Wednesday evening, June twenty-third,
eighteen hundred and ninety-seven.
109 Danforth Street,
Portland, Maine.

The Mansion served as a backdrop for Edith and William's nuptials. They wed in the flower-bedecked Parlor on June 23, 1897. More than 100 people attended the reception afterward.

The Stair Hall during the Libby years retained all of the original Morse appointments of 1860. On the staircase newel posts are two bronze torchers holding globed gas jets. After the Libbys had grandchildren and they were old enough to play in the Mansion, a favorite activity was sliding down the wide walnut handrails. Louisa placed two red plush pillows behind the statues—not to protect the sculptures but to provide a soft landing for the grandchildren's backsides. On rainy days, they also had the option of riding tricycles and bicycles around the third-floor balcony.

Mary Louise Libby Chamberlain, the second child of J.R. and Louisa, was 20 when her family took up residence at Victoria Mansion in 1894. She stayed until her marriage to Arthur Hale Chamberlain in 1899. Later in life, Mary Louise wrote a series of reminiscences about her early years, which provide wonderfully detailed and evocative glimpses into life at Victoria Mansion at the close of the 19th century.

Mary Louise's account of the sinking of the steamship *Portland* is particularly haunting. The PS *Portland* departed Boston on Thanksgiving eve 1898 and sailed into the teeth of a rapidly intensifying gale. The next morning news spread throughout the city that the ship was overdue. Mary Louise describes a period of anxious waiting: "Silence over the town became heavy and deep. . . . In the business section the shops were open but there was no trade; just in anxious questioning, 'Do you know anyone aboard?'" The *Portland* sank with nearly 200 passengers and crew, most of whom were Portland residents returning home for the holiday. Nearly everyone in the city knew someone aboard. Mary Louise recalled, "In our house, the telephone kept ringing all day, first with the news that the father and brother of one of my best friends were on the boat on their way home from Harvard. Again and again it rang, until, by night, we could count six we knew." (Courtesy of Maine Historical Society.)

The first Libby grandchild arrived in 1899, and to commemorate the event, four generations of women posed for a photograph; from left to right are great-grandmother Mary Thaxter Larrabee, Louisa's mother (1818–1910); (standing) grandmother Louisa Larrabee Libby (1845–1923); grandchild Alice Cutter (1899–1989); and mother Edith Libby Cutter (1872–1990).

Here, three Libby grandchildren pose by the Mansion's front fence about 1922. J.R. and Louisa delighted in their growing family, hosting grandchildren for visits and overnight stays. Many members of this next generation forged sentimental bonds with the house that inspired them to return original furnishings into the 21st century.

Both the Morses and the Libbys employed domestic servants, though only a handful can be identified through existing records. While their duties took them throughout the house, their main workspaces and living quarters were set apart in the ell, beyond the view of guests. Yet their relative invisibility belies the intimacy of the relationships they developed with the families they served. In this photograph taken about 1920, domestic Sabina Grady poses with a Libby grandchild on the Mansion's front steps.

Seven

INTERREGNUM

J.R. Libby died in 1917, followed by wife Louisa in 1923. They were both spared the economic cataclysm of the Great Depression, which brought about the end of the Libby store and the financial struggles that ensued. Their daughter Alice Libby Brown lived in the Mansion with her husband, Merle, until 1928. Thereafter, the main part of the house was all but mothballed, with caretakers occupying the rear wing. When upkeep on the aging mansion become increasingly expensive, the Libby children put it up for sale in 1935.

J. R. LIBBY, PROMINENT IN BUSINESS WORLD, IS DEAD

Notable Career Ends After Long Illness—Funeral to Be Thursday at 2.30

After an illness of several weeks, during much of the time confined to his bed, J. R. Libby, one of Portland's leading merchants, died late yesterday afternoon at his home on Danforth street. He was taken ill some months ago, and during much of this time he had been confined to his house, afterwards taking his bed. He took much interest in his summer place at Bonny Eagle, and it was hoped that the change which a visit there provided would prove beneficial. He spent part of the Summer there, later being removed to his home in this City. His strong constitution and indomitable will seemingly defied the illness, and for several weeks he lingered, gradually failing in recent weeks.

The funeral services will be held Thursday afternoon at 2.30 at the family residence, 109 Danforth street.

The death of Joseph R. Libby brings to a close a life of long activity in business and of intense interest in many of the moral and religious movements of his day. These years, more than half a century in business, were spent in Buxton, Boston, Biddeford, St. Louis and Portland for the most part. The greater part of the time large interests occupied his attention

J. R. LIBBY.

The great bulk of the Mansion's furnishings, including decorative objects such as glass, ceramics, and artwork, migrated to the homes of the five Libby children, who continued to care for and cherish them. Ralph G. Libby, shown here with son Daniel and daughter Ellen, brought a number of important objects to his Portland home. Thanks to the generosity of the Libby family, most of the house's exquisite furnishings made their way "home" through the ensuing decades. Ellen Libby Lawrence, shielding her eyes from the sun in this photograph, was a tireless champion for the return of the Mansion's original contents throughout her long life.

The house languished in Portland's depressed real estate market, with little to no interest shown by potential purchasers. A view of the Park Street side of the house about 1936 shows the "For Sale" sign of a Portland real estate company mounted on the lower Parlor window. Anticipating possible demolition of a costly asset that was rapidly depreciating, the Libbys began plans to have fixtures such as mirrors and gasoliers removed.

In this c. 1935 photograph, the rear of the Mansion property is beginning to fill in with vegetation, with new growth occupying the footprint of the missing side ell porch. A ladder leaning against a chimney hints at the never-ending struggle of maintaining an aging and complex building.

Caretakers occupied the Mansion off and on after the Libbys' departure, undertaking basic maintenance and keeping a watchful eye on the property. Woodbury Morrill, seen here on the front stairs during the 1947 wedding of his daughter Claire, was a resident caretaker from 1936 into the 1950s.

During the 1930s, the main part of the Mansion was all but deserted, excepting the occasional overnight stay by visiting friends and relatives. Shadows dance on the walls in this c. 1935 image of the Stair Hall. Though the house was bereft of furnishings, the painted decoration of the walls and ceilings was still in near perfect condition.

During this fraught period of the house's existence, the Historic American Buildings Survey (HABS) documented the Mansion before what everyone expected to be its demise. The Dining Room, bereft of furnishings, was a far cry from the convivial space enjoyed by the Morses and Libbys in years past.

Both the Red (shown here) and Green Bedrooms still had their massive, elegantly draped beds in place during the HABS project. They were initially left behind by the Libby children because their sheer size was not conducive to use in more modern homes. These are the only known images of the beds, as both were removed from the house shortly after this. They have never been found.

The Green Bedroom bed's elaborate hangings contained repeating *fleur de lis* motifs, a reference to the Morses' New Orleans connections. Beyond, the decoratively painted wall, with faux silk damask fabric painted in the fields of the panels, appears untouched. Most of the wall and ceiling decoration in this room was overpainted in the 1940s.

This photograph, taken around the same time as the HABS documentation, is notable in that it affords a glimpse of the original wrought-iron gates between the granite posts flanking the driveway as well as the wrought iron fencing that capped the stone retaining walls on the east and north sides of the property. Both were sacrificed to a scrap drive during World War II.

The Mansion continued to possess a magnetic allure long after its age began to show. In 1927, near the end of the Libby occupancy, noted American artist Edward Hopper painted a watercolor of the forlorn mansion, its deterioration echoed in the remains of a large dead elm tree shorn of its limbs in the foreground. (Courtesy of Harvard College.)

A photograph taken 10 years later shows the scene virtually unchanged. Note the telephone pole and street directional signs in front of the tree carcass in the photograph, details omitted by Hopper. Two additional elms, located at the far left and far right of the image, still appear relatively healthy.

A photograph taken in the spring of 1939 from the same vantage point as the preceding images shows the bulk of the dead tree is now gone. It was toppled by the Great New England Hurricane of September 1938. When it fell, its roots ripped up a large section of the front flagged sidewalk and collapsed the section of iron and granite perimeter fence behind it. The telephone pole in the foreground has been replaced, likely due to damage from the falling tree's root system; the street directional signs have been mounted higher on the pole. A keen eye will notice that the outer superstructure covering the great stained-glass stair hall skylight (immediately to the left of and behind the tower) has a number of missing and broken plate glass panels. This damage was caused by flying debris during the storm. Falling shards caused the destruction of much of the stained glass that it was meant to protect. The loss of this glass left the Stair Hall temporarily open to the elements.

Eight

Rescue and Resurrection

By the late 1930s, the house's fate was uncertain. A first attempt to save it was mounted by Portland businessman Walter Davis (1885–1966). Davis was a noted genealogist and history enthusiast and was president of the Maine Historical Society for almost 25 years. At a time when few locals recognized the significance of the Mansion, Davis spearheaded the first drive to preserve the house as a museum. (Courtesy of the Maine Historical Society.)

Historic preservation pioneer William Sumner Appleton (1874–1947) headed the largest preservation agency in New England, the Society for the Preservation of New England Antiquities. Appleton recognized the Mansion as one of the finest of its type and was persuaded by Walter Davis to join forces to raise funding to buy the house and partially endow its maintenance. Ultimately, the effort fell short. (Courtesy of Historic New England.)

By a great stroke of fortune, Dr. William Holmes (1874–1948) "chanced to happen upon the Mansion" in the summer of 1940 and purchased it with his own funds, "thinking, or rather hoping," as he later wrote, "that he could win cooperation to restore the mansion to somewhat of its former magnificence." Holmes is shown here in the Mansion's Parlor with Maine congresswoman (later US senator) Margaret Chase Smith, who visited during the summer of 1943.

From the beginning of his ownership, Holmes professed his belief that "the women of Maine should have this house as a shrine to Maine womanhood." It was he who named the structure Victoria Mansion in honor of Queen Victoria, whom he saw as "a noble woman, loving mother, and greatest woman ruler," a fitting—and famous—woman whom everyone would know. It was also probably a marketing effort to get people to the house, as it placed its reputation of importance beyond the purely local. In 1944, England's King George VI donated this painting of Osborne House, Queen Victoria's favorite residence, to the fledgling museum. Osborne House helped popularize Italianate architecture, paving the way for Victoria Mansion and other comparable buildings in America. This is the one real, if indirect, link between the British queen and the American building.

Dr. Holmes's sister Clara, a teacher of art and interior decoration in New York City, joined forces with him to clean, repair, and appropriately furnish the house to open to the public in 1940. In this group photograph taken in the Parlor in 1943 are, from left to right, Herman B. Libby, Mae Ford Haviland, James E. Barlow, and Clara. (Courtesy of the *Portland Press Herald*.)

Authenticity often gave way to the exigencies of getting the house open to the public. By 1940, the second-generation carpet in the Stair Hall—a relatively plain replacement for the elaborate 1860 chenille original—was itself beyond salvage, a victim, perhaps, of water damage sustained during the 1938 hurricane. Holmes covered the rough floorboards with rubber tile that gave the impression of diagonally laid black and white marble tiles.

In 1939–1940, for reasons not recorded, Clara Holmes directed the overpainting of the walls and some ceiling decorations in the Green Bedroom with a coat of flat white paint. It is possible she did this to better serve as a backdrop for the room as the newly rechristened "Girl's Room," which displayed Victorian girls' accessories in a background that is now viewed as an homage to 1940s decorating tastes.

The Reception Room was christened the "Music Room," and a piano and harp were installed to facilitate the use of the space for musical performances. There were often special Sunday afternoon piano recitals where one could sit in the room with a cup of tea and appreciate the music.

The original Parlor carpet was taken from the Mansion and installed in another house in the 1930s; it would not return to its rightful place for over three decades. In its place, Clara Holmes ordered a red plush pile carpet to "enhance the colors already in the room." With the exception of the pier tables and mirrors between the windows at each end of the room, no original furniture was used in the room's decoration, and Victorian-era pieces of greatly varying quality and design were arranged to suggest the parlor of a well-to-do family.

On days the house was open for tours, often given by guides dressed in "appropriate" Victorian costumes, a flag with the words "Victoria Mansion" was hung from a flagpole above the front entry. William Holmes signed the Mansion over to his sister Clara in April 1941 as a step towards placing the building in the hands of an organization that would run it as a museum. Clara then presented the Mansion to the Society of Maine Women of Achievement (later the Victoria Society of Maine Women of Achievement) in September 1943. The organization's earliest publicity for the Mansion heralded it as "the best standing example of Early Victorian Art, Architecture, and Decoration."

The organization was headed by Mae Ford Haviland (1874–1948) assisted by socially prominent women such as Katherine Hildreth (wife of Maine governor Horace Hildreth), Anna Gannett (of Gannett newspapers), and Dorothy Brewster (wife of Maine's senior US senator). The Victoria Society, as it subsequently became known, had 155 charter members.

By and large, the Victoria Society maintained the rooms as Clara Holmes had decorated them. In the Red Bedroom, a federal period portrait of an unknown woman above the bed adds a human element to the setting. Incongruously, a cradle occupies pride of place between the foot of the bed and the fireplace (out of frame at the right). There were never any infants born in or regularly cared for at the Mansion.

The Victoria Society actively raised funds for the care and operations of the house. In 1960, the society partnered with the nearby Lafayette Hotel to help raise the museum's profile in the local community. In support of this effort, members of the society hosted a luncheon in the hotel's main dining room. Notable guests included Edith Lansing Koon Sills (far left), wife of Bowdoin College president Kenneth C.M. Sills and recipient of an honorary doctor of humane letters from that institution for her charitable work. Edith took a particular interest in women's education and served as an early president of the Victoria Society. She is joined by two other identified attendees in the photograph: Matilda Hardy (second from right) and Elizabeth C. Nickels (far right).

That same year, the Lafayette Hotel's formal dinner menu featured an image of Victoria Mansion's Reception Room, which in those years was decorated and interpreted as a "Music Room." Additional information about the museum on the back of the menu drew guests' attention to the landmark a few blocks down Park Street.

A popular type of fundraiser for the Mansion was periodic flower shows in which Victorian-themed arrangements were placed throughout the house. Here, three members admire a bouquet in the Reception Room about 1960. Guests are identified, from left to right, as Priscilla Austin of Manchester, New Hampshire; Grace Ordway of Bay View, Saco, Maine; Evelyn Painchaud of Biddeford, Maine; Shirley Belanger of Saco; and Aline Neveux of Biddeford.

Claire Morrill, daughter of longtime mansion caretaker Woodbury E. Morrill, married Henry Dyson in Victoria Mansion's stair hall on July 5, 1947. This was the first wedding to take place in the Mansion in nearly 30 years. This dramatic photograph captures the bouquet toss from atop the central flying staircase.

The Mansion has always relied on a corps of volunteer docents for guided tours. In 1971, docent Kathleen Coyne (right) carries a guidebook which she shares with Alice Cutter Willman, a granddaughter of J.R. and Louisa Libby. They are both reflected in one of the Parlor's pier mirrors.

An outstanding event of 1973 was a check of support for Victoria Mansion by Britain's Queen Elizabeth II. As identified on the back of the photograph, Victoria Society president Irene Thomas and Doris DeWolfe look at the royal gift in hand.

A power group for fundraising in a capital campaign of 1983–1986, from left to right, Dodie Detmer, Charlotte Brown, Harriet Lutes, Alice Mary Pierce, and Martha Timothy, admire a pledge book recording the names of donors. Proceeds from the fund drive helped upgrade the Mansion's roof and heating system, restore the front entry portico, and repair dozens of deteriorating window sash.

Nine

Conservation and Restoration

During the first three decades of Victoria Mansion's life as a museum, volunteers charged with overseeing its care and maintenance struggled to keep pace with the building's deterioration. The tides did not really turn until the 1970s. In 1971, Victoria Mansion was named a National Historic Landmark. Two years later, when federal funds began flowing to support preservation work, Victoria Mansion partnered with Morgan Phillips, a consultant with the Society for the Preservation of New England Antiquities. Phillips, a brilliant polymath and true pioneer of architectural conservation, conducted a complete survey of the Mansion and threw himself immediately into solving the building's most pressing problems. In this image, carpenters working under Phillips's direction rebuild the Mansion's rooftop cornices and gutters in 1973.

By this point, the Mansion's brownstone front piazza was so badly deteriorated that it was in danger of catastrophic collapse. It is shown here in the mid-1970s with a network of timbers providing temporary shoring. Brownstone deterioration across the building posed a huge dilemma for the Victoria Society. With the original source quarries in Portland, Connecticut, closed since the 1930s, replacement in-kind was off the table.

Worries about falling stone led to the construction of a wooden enclosure protecting the building's front entrance. A glance at the ruined portico and tower beyond provides ample sources for concern. Visitation continued while the Victoria Society groped for long-term solutions to serious structural issues.

One answer to the brownstone dilemma was found right on the building. A rear porch—part of the building's original 1860 construction—was made from wood and sand painted to resemble brownstone. In the early 1980s, this "trick" was repeated on the front of the building. In this view of the front elevation, both the front porch and entry portico have been replaced with sand-painted wooden structures, blending seamlessly with the stone elements above.

Morgan Phillips oversaw the recreation of the missing ell porch in 1977. Combining photographic evidence with physical evidence such as the faint "ghosts" left behind wherever porch elements came into contact with the building, Phillips developed a set of complete-scale drawings for the structure. In this image, taken late that summer, the columns of the recently completed porch are still in their white primer. A later coat of sand paint turned them magically to "stone."

Superior artisans elevated the project, setting the highest standards for future work. In this view of the recreated ell porch's corner column, the quality of the carved capitals, executed by Andrew Ladygo of the Society for the Preservation of New England Antiquities, is evident. Great emphasis was placed on remaining faithful to the original elements. This began with careful measurements and drawings by Morgan Phillips. Today, Victoria Mansion maintains an archive containing all of the carved stone elements that have been removed from the building through the years. These will serve as models for the future, ensuring that artisans undertaking future restorations—perhaps decades or even centuries down the road—can refer back to original elements rather than copies.

To seal out the rain on the gentle slopes of Victoria Mansion's hipped roofs, original architect Henry Austin called for the use of terne metal, rolled iron sheets dipped in an alloy of lead and tin. If carefully installed, such roofs could last a century or more, as this one likely did. By the middle of the 20th century, however, the Mansion was plagued with intermittent leaks, a problem only briefly corrected by the installation of an inappropriate asphalt replacement roof. In 1984, Victoria Mansion called on Heritage Roofing to install a new "century roof" of flat-seamed copper. Here, the framework for the atrium protecting the skylight is being raised into place. This project made possible all the work that followed below, both inside and outside the building.

Brownstone deterioration continued to bedevil the Mansion into the 1980s. Cast stone provided another path forward. In 1988, a pilot project explored the selective replacement of deteriorated carved elements with units cast in molds taken from better-preserved elements elsewhere on the building. Here, a window sill support bracket, copied from the west side of the building, is prepared for installation on the east side.

Once in place, the new bracket blended well with the surrounding stonework. Carefully chosen pigments and aggregates ensured that the cast element successfully mimicked the surrounding brownstone. This pilot project also explored the possibility of recutting the building's massive foundation blocks into smaller units for use higher up on the building. The smooth ashlar units to the left of the bracket were cut from the base block below, which was replaced with cast stone.

The reopening of a brownstone quarry in Portland, Connecticut, marked the dawn of a new era in Victoria Mansion's restoration. Between 2004 and 2006, the museum undertook the total rebuilding of the tower and front entry stairs, all with material identical to that used in the building's original construction. The project kicked off with the removal of the tower roof, which sat on the Mansion lawn for the duration.

Christoph Henning, a traditionally trained stone carver, capped off the project with the installation of two intricately carved finials anchoring the front handrails. These were based on a single, deteriorated original that had been removed from the building decades earlier and stored in the basement. The quarry supplying stone for the project closed permanently soon thereafter.

With so many serious problems posed by the Mansion itself in the late 1970s, little thought was given to the Carriage House. It, too, was forlorn, as is evident in this 1973 photograph. By this time the building's original scored mastic coating had peeled away, exposing the brick understructure. The wooden cornice, just below the roofline, had rotted significantly. In 1984, a white knight arrived in the form of the Portland Design Team, a local architectural firm that took on the complete rehabilitation of the structure in return for a long-term lease. They outgrew the space in less than 10 years, and a buyout of the lease was offered to Victoria Mansion. Today, the restored structure serves as the visitor center and museum shop with office space above.

For more than four decades, Victoria Mansion has served as a working laboratory for the development of conservation technology. Special epoxies, formulated to accommodate the seasonal movement of exterior woodwork, have been used on the building since the 1970s, providing a new lease on life for aging wooden elements. Here, preservation woodworker John Leeke applies epoxy treatments to a deteriorated column base in 1989. It remains in service more than 30 years later.

Preservation woodworker Robert Cariddi has been caring for Victoria Mansion since the mid-1980s. He is shown here next to the Mansion's elaborately carved front doors, which he restored in 1986, replacing over 100 losses. These doors were among the few pieces of mansion woodwork originally manufactured in Portland. They were made by cabinetmaker Charles Blake in his Union Street shop.

John Leeke (left) and Caleb Hemphill (right) hold a new spire for the Carriage House cupola, recreated with the aid of photographs and physical evidence in 2003–2004. Though major challenges remained, the organization had, by this point, created enough breathing room to restore some flourishes that make the buildings so special.

During the 1990s, major improvements were made to the Mansion's grounds. Here, the property's perimeter fence is partially disassembled and waiting to receive new steel balusters, replicas of the cast-iron originals. Deterioration of the surrounding slate sidewalk also needed to be addressed by this point.

Hudson River Dark stone was selected to replace the 1860 sidewalk paving. A pile of stone sits in a yard in East Branch, New York, in 1994, awaiting shipment to the Mansion.

The City of Portland undertook the work to replace the sidewalk in-kind, improving pedestrian safety without disrupting the 19th-century ambiance of the surrounding landscape. This image, taken shortly after the completion of both sidewalk and perimeter fence, harkens back to 19th-century photographs of the streetscape.

Dutch elm disease gradually robbed Portland's streets of its stately, towering elms. In 2014, the City of Portland replaced the Mansion's three elms with blight-resistant varieties, which should reach their mature height in 25 years.

After decades of resolving major problems on the exterior of the building, the museum turned some of its energies toward interior restoration at the turn of the 20th century. Glass conservator Robin Neely is pictured at work restoring the Mansion's central stair hall skylight. Neely incorporated roughly 50 percent of the original glass that survived the 1938 hurricane, replicating the missing pieces before reinstallation in 2001.

The first major interior paint conservation project happened in 1988 under the direction of Morgan Philips. Years of coal dust and grime had accumulated on the Dining Room ceiling, obscuring a breathtaking display of the wood grainer's art beneath. This photograph captures the dramatic night-and-day contrast between cleaned and uncleaned surfaces.

In 2007–2008, the museum undertook its first whole-room restoration in the Turkish Smoking Room, a small but densely decorated space. Gianfranco Pocobene Studio led off the effort with a full conservation cleaning of the room's Islamic-inspired painted decoration. This was followed by a restoration phase, which included the in-painting of losses and the reapplication of missing gold leaf highlights.

A full restoration was achieved with the recreation of upholstery and window treatments using the 1860 originals as guides. Prelle of Lyon, France, reproduced the jacquard wool and silk fabrics. Passementerie Verrier of Paris created the intricate silk tassels and trims. The room today looks much as it did when the Morses first crossed the threshold.

Conservator Corinne Long tacks down flaking paint on the Reception Room ceiling. Between 2016 and 2018, Victoria Mansion tackled its most ambitious interior paint conservation effort to date. The Reception Room's ornate confection of cast and flat plaster, decorated with faux fabrics, trompe l'oeil moldings, and colorfully painted flowers and ornaments, took hundreds of hours to conserve. Once again, every bit of the remaining original decorative surfaces was preserved in place before cleaning. Minor losses throughout the room were carefully color matched and touched in by the conservation team, allowing the room to read as an uncompromised and cohesive whole. The results were a revelation and provided further proof of Victoria Mansion's remarkable state of preservation beneath the veil of soot deposited over the last 160 years.

Between 2019 and 2021, conservators treated decorative paint on the walls and ceiling of the Parlor, the Mansion's largest interior space save the stair hall. Two paintings on canvas depicting scenes from Homer's *Iliad* graced the Parlor ceiling for 154 years before being removed to storage in 2014 to halt their deterioration. Complete in-studio treatment included the laying down and re-attachment of flaking paint, careful cleaning, and the in-painting of numerous losses. After relining they were returned to their rightful places on the Parlor ceiling in 2020. Here, director Tim Brosnihan helps hold a canvas in place while conservator Corinne Long uses an iron to soften a heat-activated adhesive backing. Reattachment of the canvasses was the crowning touch of the two-year effort. All of the moldings immediately surrounding the canvas are two-dimensional forms painted on flat plaster. Guidicini's mastery of trompe l'oeil decoration was all the more evident after the full range of tones emerged during cleaning.

About the Organization

What is Victoria Mansion? Put the question this way and the answer will center around the building and its furnishings. To be sure, the house and its remarkable collection of Victorian decorative art is the main attraction. But one might also ask, "Who is Victoria Mansion?" Victoria Mansion is more than just the physical; it is an organization driven by individuals who have, for three successive generations, dedicated themselves to the building's preservation and given voice to its many stories. In this larger sense, Victoria Mansion is both the building and the people who care for and share it.

As an organization, Victoria Mansion has evolved significantly over the last 80 years. In the beginning, the cast was largely limited to William and Clara Holmes, who, with a small group of supporters, saved the building from demolition and opened it to the public. Under the direction of the Victoria Society for Maine Women of Achievement, Victoria Mansion was part social club and part museum, with membership limited to women. During the 1980s and 1990s, Victoria Mansion changed its trajectory, hiring its first professional staff and opening up membership to all those with an interest in the house and its history. As the organization's tent expanded, so too did its ability to tackle the preservation challenges posed by the building and to put the house and its collections into historical context for an ever-increasing number of annual visitors.

Today, Victoria Mansion is a nonprofit organization receiving the lion's share of its funding through ticket receipts and the generosity of its supporters. Victoria Mansion's two-fold mission enjoins its board, staff, and volunteers to preserve this landmark property and to use it as an educational resource to teach the visiting public about Victorian art, architecture, and history. Over the last decade, the museum has welcomed upwards of 30,000 annual visitors from all over the country and the world. For more information about the organization and its work, please visit victoriamansion.org.

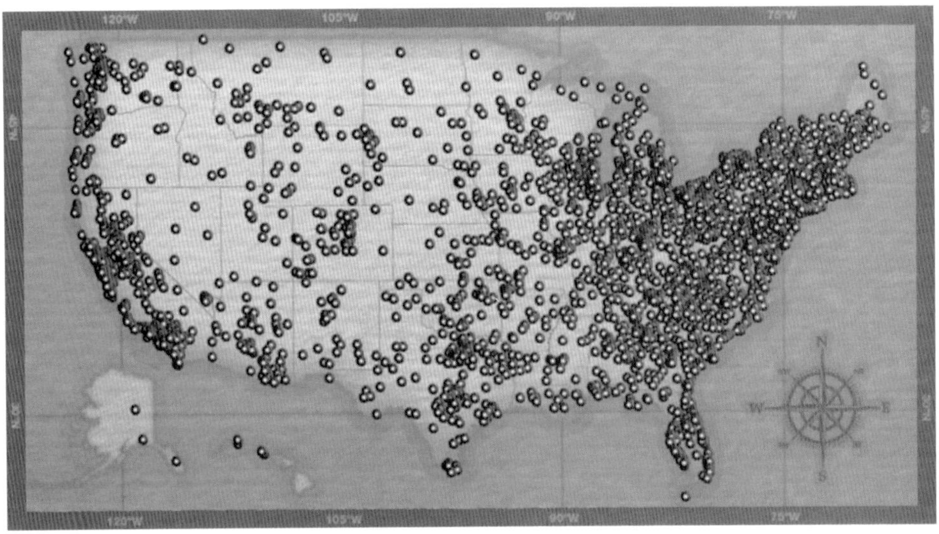